Moral Acrobatics

Moral Acrobatics

How We Avoid Ethical Ambiguity by
Thinking in Black and White

PHILIPPE ROCHAT

OXFORD
UNIVERSITY PRESS

OXFORD
UNIVERSITY PRESS

Oxford University Press is a department of the University of Oxford. It furthers
the University's objective of excellence in research, scholarship, and education
by publishing worldwide. Oxford is a registered trade mark of Oxford University
Press in the UK and certain other countries.

Published in the United States of America by Oxford University Press
198 Madison Avenue, New York, NY 10016, United States of America.

© Oxford University Press 2021

CIP data is on file at the Library of Congress
ISBN 978–0–19–005765–7

DOI: 10.1093/oso/9780190057657.001.0001

1 3 5 7 9 8 6 4 2

Printed by Sheridan Books, Inc., United States of America

Contents

PART 4: DEVELOPMENT: WHAT ARE THE ORIGINS OF OUR MORAL DECISIONS?

Story of This Book and Acknowledgments

It was under the roof of the most improbable building when I first heard that Hitler was a vegetarian. It made my head spin and planted the seed of this book. The building was an intact aristocratic 17th-century "hotel particulier" on l'ile St Louis in the heart of historic Paris. It was at the Hotel de Lauzun (see Figure 0.1), Head Office of the Paris Institute of Advanced Study (IEA). I was an invited fellow at the IEA part of the Fall 2014 and Spring of 2015. I was invited to write about lying and deception in children. I ended up also outlining this book and started to write some of its chapters.

With other lucky fellows, we met daily in this building with other residents for abundant lunch and lively interdisciplinary discussions on various topics, from collective violence to the history of diplomacy, religious warfare, the neuroscience of memory, and my topic: the developmental origins of duplicity and lying. We were treated like princes, surrounded by a devoted staff that resonated with the aristocratic surroundings. We had offices in the attic where Charles Baudelaire, Theophile Gauthier, and other 19th-century bohemian artists and poets lived, wrote, and explored artificial paradises. In all, it was indeed an appropriate location to reflect on the origins of human delusions and moral hypocrisy.

The Hotel de Lauzun is emblematic of manners of good taste and conspicuous wealth from the ancient regime of Louis the XIVth. The place where I embarked to think about deception was one of those architectural displays of enlightened power and wealth from an era where the king was equated to the sun, surrounded by gold reliefs and richly decorated paintings of naked hunting Adonis and other sensuous pies in blue skies. Those were the skies starred by 19th-century bohemian members of the so-called hashichians' club (club des hashichiens) who met at the same address to explore sensory deregulation. Again, not a bad place to explore self-delusion like phenomena.

I spent part of the 2014–2015 academic year pouring over the topic of lying and organizing interdisciplinary workshops, trying to shed some lights on the nature and function of human duplicity. In the meantime, I also agonized over the fact that Hitler was a vegetarian, so much so that I decided to use it as a departure point for a different kind of book. For weeks on end

Figure 0.1 Hotel de Lauzun, headquarter of the Paris Institute of Advanced Study.

I became obsessed with the fact. I had to think, read, and talk about it. It quickly became the melody you hate but cannot help whistling. I asked everybody around me if they knew, systematically recording responses and reactions to the question. I also toyed with the idea that it could be a catchy title for the book: "Hitler Was a Vegetarian!" as a pretext to think about it more. It became close to an obsession, and there was no end in view. So much that, in the end, I decided not to use it as a title because it was too abrasive and provocative for others, an actual repellent for an audience I wanted to engage on the issue of moral hypocrisy and its psychological origins, not on the Third Reich. Hitler's vegetarianism was not central but a good paradigm for the theme I really wanted to write about, only too briefly discussed in two preceding books.[1]

The theme revolves around the strong intuition that we are constantly impersonating and building characters depending on situations, like Dr. Jekyll and Mr. Hyde. I wanted to reflect on the very human capacity to hold multiple, often contradictory moral standards and the acrobatic ways we turn our vest, managing to wear multiple "moral hats" for one head, somehow maintaining what typical individuals experienced as self-unity. Self-unity was a good starting point to understand how we construe others as well our own values and perspectives in life, begging the question of what holds our morals together in the midst of all the hats we wear. Mother, father, son, daughter, sibling, lover, leader, follower, criminal, victim, soldier, torturer, employee, employer: master one moment, slave the next. As a developmental psychologist, I knew I wanted to write about the developmental origins of what I saw as the human fundamental ability to compartmentalize existence into multiple plays and acting roles while maintaining a unique sense of self.

This is how I ended choosing the actual title: *Moral Acrobatics*. The project led me to new territories that extended way beyond my area. I read about Nazism, torturers, criminals, and absurd gang warfare, as well as Mother Theresa. As in traveling, it gave broader, more powerful meanings to my own scientific research. What could be better?

The chapters that follow are intentionally short, realizing that contemporary readers inside and outside of academia have more and more the attention span of flies, a secular trademark in our age of impatience. The goal is to get some ideas across, as directly as possible, the main argument of the book being that we need to embrace the fact that moral ambivalence is the rule

---

[1] Rochat, P. (2009). *Others in mind: Social origins of self-consciousness*. New York, NY: Cambridge University Press; Rochat, P. (2014–2015). *Origins of possession: Owning and sharing in development*. New York, NY: Cambridge University Press.

rather than the exception. It is a cornerstone of our psychology as members of a self-conscious and symbolic species.

By acknowledging and trying to seize some of the mechanisms behind our moral ambiguities, we might be better apt at capturing what we mean by being moral or having morals. It could only help us to become more educated and just toward ourselves and others. That is the bet of this book. It is intended to be bold and to hold attention not only with short chapters, but also by removing any academic smoke screens, technical jargons, and other tedious information from the main text, all of it referred in footnotes for those interested in digging further.

The book is organized in four main parts with a comparable number of short chapters. Each part revolves around a particular moral question. Part 1 (Facts) assembles six chapters around the question "What does it mean to be moral?" Chapters point to some basic facts providing some existential framing to some of the reasons behind the inescapable ambiguities of morals tied to human self-conscious psychology. Part 2 (Proclivities) assemble seven chapters around the question "What guides our moral decisions?" These chapters point to basic psychological and predictable forces driving human morals that are source of inescapable moral hypocrisy. Part 3 (Mechanisms) has seven chapters on the question "What shapes our moral decisions?" Chapters in this section captures some of the mechanisms underlying human moral judgments, typically leading to inequity and strong biases, including major blind spots. Finally, Part 4 (Origins) include five chapters on the question "What are the origins of our moral decisions?" In this last section, the content pertains to human self-conscious psychology in the perspective of development, which include the emergence of lying and deception in children, as well as the role culture may play in shaping moral ambiguity and hypocrisy in development.

In a conclusion, I try to show how universal *moral frailty* is, revealing of the forces and tensions making us the acrobatic moral agents we are. It is the main conundrum portrayed in all enduring myths and tragedies across all cultures, as far back as recorded history goes.

In a postscript chapter, I address the issue of the human uncanny propensity toward violence, trying (just a try) to make sense of it in light our self-conscious psychology as well as our unique dependence on others.

Note that some might legitimately object my overly Western (WEIRD) perspective on human morals (Western, educated, industrial, rich, and democratic following the acronym introduced by Henrich et al., in 2010). As a

Western academic, I do own the fact that my perspective is tainted by rationalism and individualism, originating from an overwhelmingly analytical education and culture. However, let me refer readers to the last chapter ("What About Culture and Development?"), as well as the conclusion of the book ("Human Moral Frailty"). Both chapters do address the cross-cultural validity of the ideas contained in this book, acknowledging the great and varied cultural expressions of moral values, and the importance of factoring history, context, and situations to account for these expressions. However, above and beyond, I try to show that moral acrobatics and moral frailty is a core conundrum shared by members of all human societies, obviously in ways that reflect the many human ways of being together as either small or large group of individuals sharing a collective life with particular values and traditions. This core existential conundrum (human moral frailty and acrobatics) is what this book is about, above and beyond all of our great diversity in interpreting such conundrum, at both group and individual levels. I propose that this core existential conundrum is a human universal. It is an intuition helping me to create meanings as I travel, meet people, read, and navigate the social world on all corners of the planet. I trust this intuition also because it appears to stimulate interesting and fundamental questions regarding the nature of our morals, in ways that I think have been neglected by moral philosophers and social scientists, but fully acknowledged by literary giants like Cervantes, Shakespeare, and Dostoevsky. It is also the theme of human moral frailty that seems to feed all ancestral tales, from Japanese Noh, ancient Greek tragedies, the Indian Ramayana, and all the recorded oral tales and rituals of preindustrial small-scale human societies from around the world. In my view, its universal validity is difficult to overlook, but you the reader will be the ultimate judge. Ideas contained in this book are meant to start a conversation, not to close it, and if it does, be it only in the mind of the reader, the book will have achieved its main goal.

Let me acknowledge those who supported me in this writing enterprise: the IEA, its staff, and warm director Gretty Mirdal for all of their generosity; Alain Berthoz of the Collège de France who sponsored my stay at the IEA as a fellow during the 2014–2015 academic year; and all the other IEA fellows during that year who shared with me their knowledge and research expertise in their field.

My thanks extend to Emory University, my home institution for the past 28 years for its continuing support in protecting my research freedom, and to the staff and numerous students of the Emory Infant and Child Laboratory who somehow managed to adjust to my ways of doing research, often taking me far off typical academic tracks and schedules.

Michael Heller, my faithful, always inspiring friend from teen age who read earlier drafts and—as usual—provided untamed and astute criticisms, sharing his encyclopedic and well assimilated breath of knowledge.

Finally, to all the people and friends I met, inside and well outside of academia, often by chance encounters while traveling in remote places. I used you as sounding board and critics of my ideas and certainly borrowed some of them from you. The list would be too long, and I know I must have forgotten many of you, met while cultivating the art of drifting and roaming this incredibly fascinating place that is now as we live.

This book is for Rana Rochat, the least moral acrobat I've ever encountered.

Introduction

Moral Battlefield and the Illusion of Moral Unity

> Beauty is mysterious as well as terrible.
> God and devil are fighting there,
> and the battlefield is the heart of man.
> —Fyodor Dostoevsky, The Brothers Karamazoff

> Take your practiced powers and stretch them out until they span
> the chasm between contradictions . . .for the god wants to know
> himself in you
> —Rainer Maria Rilke, "As Once the Winged Energy of Delight"

Ahmad Rahami was arrested for detonating a pipe bomb on 23rd Street in
New York City. After a bloody chase, rounds of gunfire exchanges, and two
policemen hit, he was eventually shot down and caught in New Jersey where
he lives with his family. For many years, he managed a family business with
his father and brothers called First American Fried Chicken, a popular fast-
food joint on a busy street in nearby Elizabeth.

Learning about the arrest, a regular patron of First American Fried
Chicken was stunned. Interviewed by journalists in search of cues about
Rahami as a person, he bursts out, saying, "He's a very friendly guy; he gave
me free chicken. . . . He was always the most friendly man you ever met."[2]
A strikingly different image of Rahami emerges from this statement—the ac-
quaintance having trouble reconciling the image of the friendly, generous,
and warm individual he genuinely experienced with the image of an actual
terrorist. Based on one, albeit particularly heinous crime, the individual is
demonized in our heads, becoming the representation of a one-dimensional
outcast. Our quick, almost reflex-like propensity to demonize people, or
inversely to lift them to unrealistic degrees of veneration, does not require

[2] Schweber, N., & Remnick, N. (2016, September 19). A suspect with a taste for fast cars. *New York Times*..

Moral Acrobatics. Philippe Rochat, Oxford University Press (2021). © Oxford University Press.
DOI: 10.1093/oso/9780190057657.001.0001

particularly malicious, heinous, or uncommon heroic acts. One sentence, one clumsy judgment, one word, one ill public thought, one sexual slip of the tongue can tumble someone's reputation. A love infatuation, a word, a gesture can destroy one's own public trust, sometimes with major geopolitical consequences.[3]

Take US Senator Gary Hart of Colorado who had a good shot at becoming president in the 1980s. In two campaigns for the White House, he tumbled twice by being accused of lust and womanizing. Hart was a serious Democratic contender. Had he managed better his sensuous indulgence, 20th-century's fate might have been very different. The lust indulgence of an otherwise highly qualified individual to become very powerful ended up being the central piece of his political demise. Same for Bill Clinton, who was almost impeached in his second term at the helm of the world's largest economy and military power for lusting with a young intern fresh out of college.

The kind of stark incongruence between facts and first-hand experience with individuals, the discrepancy between what happens behind closed doors, what acquaintances know of a person and what is inferred from a transgression in the public eye, is not unusual. Intimates typically have a hard time reconciling the persons they know and the heinous crimes they are suddenly accused of. "Impossible, they've got the wrong guy" is a common comment from family members and neighbors of the arraigned, telling much about the ways we come to form impressions about people and our own ambivalence in judging others. Hollywood plays on such ambivalence. The phenomenal success of mafia movies or series like *Breaking Bad* rests primarily on our fascination for double-faced characters who on the inside promote values we can all relate to such as protection, loyalty, affection, love, and decency within the family circle and in the meantime are ring leaders of the most terror-filled and vicious crime systems on the outside. Such moral ambivalence tickles our imagination. It fascinates, and we end up spending a lot of time and money contemplating and reflecting upon it, always on the lookout for sensational revelations. It is the driving force behind the information industry; ask any journalist.[4]

---

[3] The 2014 movie *Force Majeure* by Swedish director Ruben Östlund is a remarkable reflection on how one very furtive, spontaneous self-protective gesture by a loving father on vacation with wife and kids can destroy the dynamic of an otherwise perfectly happy and functioning family.

[4] For those understanding French, watch the remarkable lecture on "espérer l'imprévu" (hoping for the unexpected) by Laurent Joffrin, brilliant journalist and editor of the French daily newspaper *Liberation*. Joffrin eloquently makes the bottom-line psychological point that the whole information

These observations capture in a nutshell something that is fundamental to how we construe others, value them—including ourselves—in terms of morals. Our views on people are overly simplifying, caricatures at best. They reveal the conflicting, often contradictory nature of our fluctuating values, with their own blind spots depending on context and circumstances.

What defines a person's standards of thoughts, beliefs, and behavior, here referred to as morals, are indeed highly context dependent.[5] What we think of people, the impressions we have of them cannot and never do encompass all of their multiple existential spheres. And each of us have many different existential spheres, multiple circles of valued others with whom we co-exist and interact: blood family, friends, co-workers, teammates, anonymous business partners, political affiliates. Those tend to form well-compartmentalized existential spheres, with particular roles and expectations, as well as trust attached to them. Similarly, we embody different standards depending on whom we are dealing with parents, children, priests, bosses, close friends, judges, teachers, or anonymous individuals in daily transactions.

Our standards of behavior adjust to these various rapports and roles carrying their own specificity and dictating different interactive rules and roles. Our morals are indeed highly *compartmentalized*. They are marked by the remarkable ability to switch moral codes, embodying radically different moral standards of behavior depending on circumstances and within our various existential spheres. This phenomenon forces us to shed a new light on what we mean by being moral and what unifies our morals and question the unity of moral identity and our perspective or "standpoint" in moral

---

industry rests on a universal hoarding instinct for revelations of the unexpected (http://www.gypsy-colloque.com/conference/laurent-joffrin-esperer-limprevu/).

[5] This perspective resonates with situationist views on morality, espoused in particular by moral philosopher John Doris in his book *Lack of Character* (Cambridge, England: Cambridge University Press, 2002). Doris develops the idea that social circumstances dictate morals, referring to the numerous social psychology studies demonstrating flip-flopping morals of individuals according to situations and social pressures; see, for example, the Milgram obedience or Zimbardo prisoner experiments. Note that these experiments have recently been revisited and accused of being flawed. Nonetheless, human conformity and obedience are real phenomena (see any propaganda movies from contemporary North Korea or any military boot camp around the world). Their validity, magnitude, and causes are still debated, not their existence. What Doris does not fully account for is what counts as "situation" for individual moral agents and the moral acrobatics that depend on particular spherical alliances that this book tries to take on (see Doris's 2018 target article, Doris, J. M. (2018). Précis of talking to our selves: Reflection, ignorance, and agency. *Behavioral and Brain Sciences, 41*, e36, and our follow-up commentary in the same issue, Beal, B., & Rochat, P. (2018). Innate valuation, existential framing, and one head for multiple moral hats. *Behavioral and Brain Sciences, 41*, e38.

space following philosopher Charles Taylor's construal of the self.[6] This is something too rarely considered in both moral philosophy and moral psychology that I would like to bring forth. Our morals are indeed full of blatant contradictions, with the questions being, How do we somehow manage to bring it all together in our head and how do we develop such standard juggling ability? What's behind our moral rationale(s), the apparent unity experienced of who we are as moral agents and that we assume is publicly perceived?

Just before planting his pipe bomb in a dumpster to kill presumed sinners and other innocent people in Chelsea, Rahami might well have tenderly put his kids to bed, kissed his wife and kissed his father on his forehead with respect, and then shown devotion to Allah by praying at the neighborhood mosque. Our morals do fluctuate depending on circumstances. Again, they depend on the various roles or characters we play in our existence: father, son, boss, soldier, drill sergeant. Multiple hats for one head, with the question being, What constitutes this head? Is it the sum total of all the hats? Since our standards of behavior—our *morals*—tend to fluctuate accordingly, it begs the question of what mechanisms hold our morals together as we constantly oscillate from one to another depending on the multiplicity of our social spheres. How can one be a loving father, husband, and churchgoer one moment and an atrocious rapist, criminal, and torturer, the next? That is the question, put here in extreme yet representative terms.

We might be praying around a dinner table and volunteering at church at one point. In the next, we might be sitting in a comfy chair at a desk in the military base where we work, guiding drones with a joystick to kill people somewhere in the Middle East, some of them likely to be innocents. From this perspective, we are not that different from Rahami. What is different is just that most of us don't go to the extreme of heinous terrorist acts, extermination, distal bombing, pervert kidnapping, or blind fanaticism. We refrain from showing an extreme bundle of contradictory values across existential spheres. Most of us are better at juggling our existential spheres within the limits of what is tolerated by the law.

Yet the law, universally, allows for parochialism and favoritism. It tolerates often screaming imbalances and contradictions in our morals, albeit in

---

[6] [B]eing a self is inseparable from existing in a space of moral issues, to do with identity and how one ought to be. It is being able to find one's standpoint in this space, being able to occupy a perspective in it"; Taylor, C. (1989). *Sources of the self: The making of the modern identity*. Cambridge, MA: Harvard University Press, p. 112.

variable proportions. In all human societies since beginning of recorded history, maybe with some exceptions among small bands of hunter-gatherers,[7] individuals are allowed to create substantial inequity of resources and services by amassing wealth and power that is directly transmittable to the same blood lineage. In all human societies, strict inheritance laws protect such favoritism. More generally, rare are those individuals who are de facto strict abiders to the law; most are always somehow trying to get ahead of what is tolerated by the law. Rare are the ultrastrict law abiders. The fact is that in all countries giving as little as possible to the taxman is a national sport. We tend to preserve and defend our privileges with little to no restrains and hold on to our inherited wealth and privileges as if we were naturally entitled to them. In our head, we are all monarchs chosen from above.[8]

Being entitled monarchs and the jugglers of multiple existential spheres lead us toward major flaws in our moral compass. Moral blind spots and lies are inevitable, some obviously more blatant than others. The hypocrisy of a Madoff is incomparable to Mr. Jones cheating on his tax return. However, in either case, the boundaries of moral decency are stretched. It is never possible to be completely "clean" and honest with ourselves. Those who claim to the contrary lie and should raise deep suspicion. Although trivial and for the most part unspoken, we rarely acknowledge our propensity to simplify both others and ourselves in our moral judgments and decisions. When digging below the surface, they tend to be always embedded in deeper contradictions.

Unlike most characters in Shakespeare's plays or Dostoevsky's novels, we are not inclined to acknowledge the unsettling fact that we are all made of a bundle of conflicting values. Monsters only exist in our simplifying head. Our puzzlement toward Mr. Rahami and other criminals—when going

---

[7] See, for example, Marlowe, F. W. (2010). *The Hadza: Hunter-gatherers of Tanzania*. Berkeley, CA: University California Press. The book provides a detailed ethnography of most extreme egalitarianism in resource distribution, however not overriding intrinsic inequities regarding gender and physical attributes, as well as the potential for inequal individual possessions. In my 2014 *Origins of Possession* book (Cambridge, MA: Cambridge University Press) in which I review this work, I note: "In the Hazda immediate return and highly egalitarian socio-economic system that would be most resembling our prehistoric ancestors, we can conclude that possession experience is a fact that cannot be obliterated, defining a lesser level, tamer expression of possessiveness compared to what is found in other delayed return cultures where competition is more pronounced" (p. 253).

[8] We somehow tend to overlook the crucial factor luck plays in our destiny, what we so readily experience as entitlement, including our birth, inherited wealth, good looks, intelligence, and manners, neglecting the fact that all, aside from chance, are also products of social selection and class distinction over historical time. For more evidence, see sociologist Pierre Bourdieu's 1984 classic on *Distinction: A Social Critique of the Judgment of Taste* (New York: Routledge) and also the more recent essay by moral philosopher Neil Levy: Levy, N. (2011). *Hard luck: How luck undermines free will and moral responsibility*. Oxford, England: Oxford University Press.

beyond their heinous acts—shows our difficulty in reconciling hate with the potential for love within one individual. Yet they appear to necessarily co-exist and are co-defined like night and day, figure and ground. We can't help dichotomizing individuals and group individuals into either/or in terms of absolutely distinct antinomical categories: good person versus bad person, in-group versus out-group. By dealing with these antinomical categories as normatively separate, we resist considering both, at least psychologically speaking, as mutually defined and functionally inseparable like the two sides of the same coin. The categorical (i.e., absolute) good life discussed by moral philosophers may exist as metaphysical (meta-psychological) norms to pro-duce rules and laws of justice, above and beyond what individuals experience psychologically in everyday life. As norms, they might represent meaningful guidelines, yet with no true psychological equivalent on how individuals and groups of individuals do actually battle trying to create coherence for them-selves in everyday life.

One way to account for this is the basic fact that we create meanings and feed our thoughts by creating conceptual contrasts. This is a fundamental principle of how our categorical mind works: by elimination and subtrac-tion, thinking of the world in black and white. It is also the source of many shallow judgments that are inherently flawed and incomplete. The basic pro-cess of creating meanings about people and things via highlighted contrasts in our tendency to parse the world into categories and generate opinions based on these categories leads us invariably toward rigid shortcuts, implicit biases, unwarranted prejudices, and generalizations. We talk about Chinese, Russians, or Arabs with no nuances or any obvious awareness of the multi-plicity of cultures and languages represented by such grouping. It is source of much unwarranted and highly consequential political judgments and decisions on what separates *us* from *them*. From such generalizations we build caricatures of the world around us, including ourselves. For example, in our head, we reconstruct the passage of time, which, in essence, is con-tinuous, into discrete, discontinuous "meaningful" moments like anniversa-ries. But such mental reconstructions are transforming reality, reducing its complexity, and invariably deforming it. They provide convenient shortcuts and placeholders, but they are flawed, resting on oversimplifications and resulting in prejudices toward both others and the self. This reconstructive process is essentially how our brains create meanings that feed and give trac-tion to both our thoughts and decisions. Such a process is evident at all levels, from basic perception to politics. It is at the core of how the mind works. At the level of moral decisions, this process translates into the creation of convenient norms for ourselves.

Here, I want to argue that what drives us toward our incomparable delusion and self-deception is our combined need for coherence and our propensity toward reduction. We conveniently reconstruct what end up being caricatures of others as well of who we are as moral entities. In the midst of all our documented ability to do good, to empathize, and to cooperate with others, we also live off lies, deception, systematic oversight by elimination, and, yes, downright destructiveness. This is also the darker side of who we are as a uniquely abstract and symbolic species.

There is indeed a dark side to human empathy and cooperation that needs to be acknowledged. Likewise, there is also a necessary bright side, a redeeming aspect behind the human propensity toward hate and violence. Dehumanized monsters do not exist but in our flawed head. Ultimately, I would argue that this acknowledgment is required if we want to become better and more just people. It is also a necessity if we want to become more encompassing in our theories of how our *morals* actually work.

As Dostoyevsky describes it, good and evil are always in a battlefield within the individual or group of individuals (see previous quote). This idea drives the book, the question being, What is the dynamic and how do we manage our moral battles, what consequences do they have, and how—in the end—do these battles become intrinsic to our moral judgments?

Criminals are never just criminals; good people are never just good people. This state of things is deeply incompatible with the either/or, black or white, good or bad contrasts driving our moral intuitions and righteous mind. Parochial at heart.[9] we juggle multiple standards, somehow without collapsing under the weight of our moral contradictions. Moral acrobats and norm "bricoleurs," we somehow manage to balance standards from proximal to more distal moral spheres. Distal spheres give more room for dehumanization, making us behave more fearful and defensive. It leads us toward murky zones of blind favoritism and injustice acceptance, fanciful sense of entitlement, prejudice, and other arbitrary ostracism: all of which makes us stray from the good, whatever it might mean, in absolute or relative terms such as good as opposed to bad deeds, worse as opposed to better deeds. As a

---

[9] For a recent account on the origins of parochialism and what drives the distinction between "us" and "them," see Greene, J. (2013). *Moral tribes*. New York, NY: Penguin Press, an illuminating and compelling book that combines philosophy and new findings in burgeoning field of moral neuroscience.

species, we share with other social animals a deep instinctive commitment to protect and foster intimacy with our in-group—in particular, our progenies. However, human self-conscious psychology brings love and commitment to incomparable levels of moral ambivalence. In many ways, it is our poisoned gift from Nature.

In sum, we have to acknowledge such compartmentalized moral reality, which is a neglected aspect of human moral sciences. Let us try to recognize and account for it, eventually try to own up to it. But where to start? With some basic facts attached to human unique self-conscious psychology and some of the inescapable awareness of existential certainties framing our thoughts and morals. Among those are both implicit and explicit "cursed" awareness, explaining the frailty of our morals: (1) the awareness of our own transient living state, our own mortality; (2) the role of luck and the awareness of unsurmountable inequalities among ourselves—this in spite of all our efforts to tame or ignore them; and (3) our deep dependence on others to survive both physically and psychologically. The opening chapter that follows lays out these facts trying to provide some existential framing to the psychology behind our moral acrobatics. This chapter is the first of seven (Part I: Facts), all dealing with basic facts that are central to human moral psychology, and all revolving around the question "What does it mean to be *moral*?

The next series of seven chapters deal with the question of what guides our moral decisions in terms of proclivities (Part 2); what shapes them in terms of identifiable mechanisms (Part 3); and, finally, what their origins are in the perspective development and culture (Part 4). The conclusion and postscript of the book tries to make sense of human malice, violent proclivities, and our moral vagaries as a perversion of what is fundamentally good in all of us, such as the self-sacrificing love for progenies.

PART 1

FACTS

What Does It Mean to Be "Moral"?

I sometimes like to daydream that if we were all somehow simultaneously outed as lechers and perverts and sentimental slobs, it might be, after the initial shock of disillusionment, liberating. It might be a relief to quit maintaining this rigid pose of normalcy and own up to the outlaws and monsters we are.

We Learn Nothing, Tim Kreider

1

Human Self-Reflective Curse

In the first sentence of his metaphysical essay *The Myth of Sisyphus*, Albert Camus writes: "There is but one truly serious philosophical problem, and that is suicide." Such an existential dilemma is exclusive to humans, the self-conscious signature of our species, endowed with the curse and freedom to reflect upon the meaning of their own life and situation in the universe. Sheep herds might jump off cliffs, and large mammals might beach themselves to their death, but not out of existential self-reflection and rumination.

So, how do we cope with such a self-reflective curse? We do so mainly by faking reality and tricking ourselves. We simplify, create order in our head where there is none, give ourselves illusions of control, reduce unmanageable complexities by building shortcuts, staging and challenging ourselves, dramatizing, and representing situations to enhance our embodied experience of being. We are ceaselessly creating comfort values for ourselves and for those we identify as extension of ourselves, namely in-group "family" allies. Without such propensities for creating comfort values, we would be paralyzed and unable to adjust. We all share the basic need for protection and resource security, not only for ourselves but also for those we identify with (parents, children, teammates, and other close affiliates).

As we monitor our current situation in the social world, always on the lookout for what is going to happen next, our primary concern is typically maintaining our own self-reflecting and self-edifying *zone of comfort*: pay our bills, save our assets, and the assets of those we project into. What matters first is our subjective and embodied sense of well-being, the control over our proximal and distal social environment, our own reputation and that of our kin group with whom we feel affiliated, the maintenance of close proximity and intimacy, and the struggle for recognition from others. All of it is driven primarily by in-group biases, a universal propensity toward in-group favoritism and parochialism.

The self-consciousness that is unique to our species condemns us to become Janus-faced: Dr. Jekyll and Mr. Hyde, juggling multiple standards depending on the social situation we are dealing with. We are moral acrobats.

Moral Acrobatics. Philippe Rochat, Oxford University Press (2021). © Oxford University Press.
DOI: 10.1093/oso/9780190057657.003.0001

Yet, in the meantime, because coherence is necessary to build trust in others, we profoundly despise Janus-faced ambiguity and other hypocrisies. We can't stand hypocrisy and attitude flip-flopping in others as it promotes uncertainty. Yet attitude flip-flopping is inescapable. Love always carries with it the potential for commensurate, and often incommensurate, hate and revengeful acts. The flip side of protection and love is killing when in jeopardy. This represents a central existential knot at the core of our moral psychology, the source of classic tragedies that pass the test of time, from Sophocles (i.e., *Antigone*) to Shakespeare (i.e., *Richard III*) and Dostoyevsky (i.e., *Crime and Punishment*).

Among the worst criminals are also good fathers and good mothers capable of much love for their children and other family members. Inversely, good people are potentially capable of acts of incommensurate atrocities. The reputed honest person and most caring mother can also show much violent favoritism and aggression, if for example their young, compatriots, team, or country are threatened or under attack. Yet it is an aspect of our psychology that it is not considered enough in building theories of moral psychology that would account for how we manage double standards and moral ambivalences, all mainly driven by our propensities toward nepotism and in-group favoritism. To some degree, we all end up being Dr. Jekyll and Mr. Hyde, begging the question of what might be the psychological determinants of such moral acrobatics.

It appears that moral hypocrisy and duplicity are the rule rather than just exceptions. Both are inseparable from self-consciousness and humans' unique concern for reputation. It is linked to face-maintenance (keeping apparent moral self-unity) in the midst of obvious contradictions. Powerful examples abound, such as the fact that Ben Franklin and Thomas Jefferson owned slaves or that Hitler was a vegetarian. We are indeed moral acrobats, and this has its roots in self-consciousness, the pillar of our human nature. It is also associated with the adaptive successes of our species, surviving and cooperating on all four corners of this planet, for better or for worse. Our self-conscious psychology accompanies the projection of ourselves as living entity into the past and into the future, it forces obsessive calculation and maintenance of how we are perceived by others, our reputation (from the Latin verb *putare*, to calculate or to compute). It forces us to constantly focus on others to capture their reflection of our own social worth, others as "looking glass self" following Charles Horton Cooley's, Herbert Mead's, or Erwin Goffman's original views.

Self-conscious psychology leads toward obligatory existential rumina-tion of deeply unsettling existential truths. These truths shape our moral sense, in particular what we feel and construe as right or wrong and what we experience and reason as just or unjust. Three realizations are particular determinants of our morals.

There is the awareness of our own mortality and that everything we expe-rience is transient and essentially doomed to disappear from the surface of this earth. This existential truth is the natural source of human deep, unset-tling existential angst and despair, the inescapable sense of absurdity. It is also the human universal struggle to find meanings allowing us to transcend the realization of our doom on earth. This struggle is the main existential framing of our morals.

From self-reflective rumination comes also the realization that we are born more or less privileged, by chance, a chance that gives each of us rela-tive health, beauty, and wealth. We know that this is determined by Nature's roulette outcome, whether or not God is the croupier. The inescapable real-ization of this truth makes merit deeply elusive and our strong sense of en-titlement, the fruit of our own ideas and imagination, at best. This explains human peculiar struggle with envy and our peculiar inclination toward the cultivation of resentment and revengeful violence.

Last but not least, self-reflective rumination makes us realize how de-pendent we are on others, how elusive our own freedom is because most of what we do is to please others to get their validation and how much we de-pend on how others perceive and evaluate us on our own reputation. This self-reflective rumination leads us toward the constant preoccupation with our own social place and situation, how we compare with others. Social emotions like guilt and shame, but also hubris, pride, and contempt, shape human morals. These emotions are presumably unique to human self-conscious psychology. All arise from our self-reflective propensity, framing and motivating our moral decisions. These emotions are linked to the deep-seated existential realization that without others, we are nothing. The curse of such realization is the deepest fear of being rejected and, as a consequence, a fear that makes all of us desperate for social recognition and validation, obsessed with how we are perceived and evaluated by others. Above all, we care about our own reputation. We literally exist through our good relations and cares from others, without which we deteriorate and die, both physically and psychologically. At a deep motivational level, what drives human self-conscious psychology and shapes human morals is our basic affiliation need

(BAN), with the necessary association of the deep, universal fear of being rejected by others.[1] This is the basic foundation of our insatiable need and struggle for social recognition, the human care for reputation, and our universal quest for positive evaluation from others. Think of the exponential infatuation with social medias like Facebook or Instagram, catering "thumbs up" as global commodity. In a recent epidemic, young Japanese adults meet anonymously on the Internet to arrange and set a date to commit suicide together. This strange phenomenon upholds the basic premise that people need people, even facing the most intimate and decisive of all problems: one's own death.[2] Until the end, we need the validation of others as part of our self-conscious psychology.

As Sartre wrote, "hell is other people." It is our curse to depend on others the way we do, constantly seeking for approval and validation, obsessed with the rumination of how others perceive us, what is the state of our reputation. BAN is something we share with other social animals. Human self-conscious psychology, however, brings BAN to incomparable levels of complexity, symbolism, and in the way we somehow manage double standards while maintaining self-unity and the appearance of good conscience in the face of blatant contradictions. History is replete with famous examples.

[1] See Rochat, P. (2009). *Others in mind.* Cambridge, England: Cambridge University Press.

[2] Ozawa-de Silva, C. (2008). Too lonely to die alone: Internet suicide pacts and existential suffering in Japan. *Culture Medicine Psychiatry, 32,* 516–551. Ozawa-de Silva, C. (2010). Shared death: Self, sociality and internet group suicide in Japan. *Transcultural Psychology, 47*(3), 392–418.

2

Double Standards

Ending his first inaugural term as US president (1793), Washington signed the first fugitive slave law, which allowed fugitives to be seized in any state, tried and returned to their owners. Anyone who harbored or assisted a fugitive faced a $500 penalty and possible imprisonment.[1] Now read the preamble of the US Constitution (1776): "We hold these truths to be self-evident: That all men are created equal; that they are endowed by their Creator with certain unalienable rights; that among these are life, liberty, and the pursuit of happiness."

Memorized by most US school children, this is the forceful enlightened premise of the July 4, 1776 declaration of sovereignty and independence of the United States. It was signed by 56 delegates of the 13 American colonies, including Benjamin Franklin and Thomas Jefferson, the two epitome Founding Fathers of an independent United States of America. Of the 56 signers, however, 41 owned slaves, including the latter two. As one famous song goes, "all lies and jest, still a man hears what he wants to hear, and disregards the rest."[2]

In private, George Washington is said to have opposed slavery. His accounting notes, however, show that he made his last slave purchase in 1772, and by 1774 he actually paid taxes on 135 slaves. Just one year short of the Declaration of Independence (1775), Washington offered reward for the capture and return of two runaway white servants. He also became the first president of the United States for two terms, from 1789 to 1797.[3]

The question is how we, George Washington included, so extraordinarily manage to bear such flagrant moral inconsistencies, able to tolerate for self

---

[1] Haworth, P. L. (2004/1915). *George Washington: Farmer*. Whitefish, MT: Kessinger, pp. 78–80. Dunbar, E. A. (2015, February 16). George Washington, slave catcher. *New York Times*. Retrieved from https://www.nytimes.com/2015/02/16/opinion/george-washington-slave-catcher.html.

[2] Simon, P. (1974). The boxer [Recorded song]. In *Paul Simon in Concert: Live Rhymin'* [Album]. New York, NY: Columbia.

[3] How many signers of the Declaration of Independence owned slaves? *Mr.Heintz.com*. Retrieved from http://www.mrheintz.com/how-many-signers-of-the-declaration-of-independence-owned-slaves.html.

Moral Acrobatics. Philippe Rochat, Oxford University Press (2021). © Oxford University Press.
DOI: 10.1093/oso/9780190057657.003.0002

and make tolerable for others electing him, such obvious ideological dissonance and inconsistencies? What are the mechanisms behind such tolerance,
allowing powerful individuals to embody screaming contradictions while
seemingly avoiding the stress of cognitive dissonance? How does anyone
manage to live in apparent good conscience while bearing such blatant moral
inconsistencies? There seems to be only one feasible explanation. The world
must be somehow reconstructed in our head, transformed in imagination
to become morally reasonable, more manageable and justifiable, for self and
for others, especially for those brought to power and looked upon for their
moral authority.

Hitler, the guy who orchestrated the systematic killing of millions, was a
vegetarian, a vocal hater of meat eaters and sport hunters, promulgating laws
to prevent pain in animals. From the prototype of Mad and Bad, how is that
possible? How, in his head and in ours, can we reconcile the prototypical incarnation of evil with any potential consideration for life and some kind of
genuine love for Nature?

There are multiple reasons for being a vegetarian and refusing to eat meat.
There are also different ways of being a vegetarian, from strict vegan to just
occasional fish eater. It can be for health and digestive reasons or for deep
personal disgust toward flesh or eating anything that has eyes. It can also
be based on loftier grounds like religion, politics, and fight against global
warming given that animals raised for their meat produce more carbon mon-
oxide emission than cars.[4] We typically tend to associate vegetarianism with
a person's deliberate stance toward Nature, the index of her moral stance
and conscientiousness toward other animals. Framed like this, learning
that Hitler was a vegetarian is unsettling for most and a strong case of moral
incongruity.

If you are not a World War II history buff and don't know much about
Nazi ideology, it is difficult to make sense of Hitler's vegetarianism. For most
people, it is an odd, unsettling historical fact. My experience shows that for
a few smarty-pants, learning for the first time that Hitler was a vegetarian is
not really surprising and unsettling. I observed that for these in-the-know
people, there is no obvious reasons to attribute a causal link between the

[4] "The United Nations Food and Agriculture Organization estimates that livestock production is
responsible for 14.5% of global greenhouse gas emissions, more than all the cars, trucks, planes, and
ships in the world!" Schwartz, S. (2017). 5 facts about animal agriculture and air pollution that you
just can't argue with. *One Green Planet*. Retrieved from https://www.onegreenplanet.org/environ-
ment/facts-about-animal-agriculture-and-air-pollution/.

refusal to eat meat and a nonviolent ethic. The refusal to eat meat is not necessarily associated with nonviolence. For the majority of individuals, however, which included me, that such a short-cut assumption prevailed led to
strong dismay.

The majority reaction regarding Hitler's vegetarianism captures something
essential about our morals. It reveals that for the majority of us there is an inclination toward overly simplistic and categorical ways of judging the morals of
others, typically in black and white, either/or, or knee-jerk eliminative terms,
leaving little to no room for skepticism and critical thinking—no room for
the pondering of Hitler's moral acrobatics, his compartmentalized montage
of ethical values. The deduction is based on quick heuristics and associative
shortcuts, quasi-automatic deductions taken for absolute, either/or normative
truths: Hitler was a vegetarian? A profound oxymoron, a blatant contradiction,
a moral absurdity deduced from our majority categorical inclination to think
the world in black and white, good or bad terms with no shades of grey.

We are quick to perceive moral inconsistencies in others, yet manage to
live our own blatant contradictions, masked with personal montage of apparent good conscience. In defense of our children, we fall for strong and
unfair biases. By either omission or commission, we conceal inconvenient
truths and minimize, and often block out, moral inconsistencies to brand
ourselves and those we identify with.

Parochialism is universally irresistible, and we kid ourselves as well as
others regarding the unity and consistency of our own morals. In reality,
we cannot escape holding multiple standards depending on both situation
and degree of affiliation. There is indeed much delusion and blind oversights
regarding what we experience as our own moral consistency and how we
perceive and judge the moral consistency of others, the categorical way we
experience our own moral self and the moral self of others.

Popes and other leaders get beatified for defending the poor, the meek,
and the oppressed, while spending their lives in the most lavish environment,
surrounded by immense wealth, notwithstanding a crowd of servitudes and
submissions. At a smaller scale, we all live to the detriment and servitude
of some. Class and caste systems exist in various forms across all cultures.
Some are born beautiful, and others, ugly. A bottom-line truth is that there is
no fair world, and this pushes us toward unavoidable moral inconsistencies,
despite constant political efforts at mitigating such an unfair state of things.
The world is unfair and makes moral acrobatics inescapable. It constrains us
toward moral montages.

The question is, How do we cope with such an unfair state of things? How do we build good conscience while protecting and maintaining privileges for ourselves and intimate affiliates, with questionable merit attached to those privileges that we feel so naturally entitled to? How do we, in good conscience, live with the have-less and those who are more well off than us because of the lottery of their birth? How did I manage this morning to pass nonchalantly this emigrant family with young children laying frozen on a yellow mildewed rotten foam mattress, looking down at them without blinking on my way to the cozy old Parisian library to continue writing about moral ambivalence and hypocrisy? What kind of acrobatics am I to maintain and face to manage moral coherence in the midst of so much injustice and obviously unfair discrepancies?

A straightforward answer is that to avoid implosion under the weight of moral inconsistencies and blatant ambiguities, we are forced to operate along multiple, typically well-compartmentalized moral standards. We switch moral codes depending on people and situations, rarely losing the sense of our own moral unity. We grow to become very apt at juggling multiple standards. We are moral acrobats always about to lose balance, while dancing over shaky moral montages and other bricolages: "something constructed or created from a diverse range of available things" (*Oxford English Dictionary*).

3

Moral Acrobats

We juggle multiple hats on a single head making the issue of morality particularly complex. We switch from being Dr. Jekyll in one moment, Mr. Hyde the next; from loving father, to abusive boss, for example. Morality, psychologically speaking, is essentially the balancing of opposite propensities that co-exist and are co-defined within us as individuals, but also as groups of individuals: the propensity to do good or bad, act selfishly or for the common good. The good always tends to hide the bad, and vice versa. The good expressed in a person *only* exists and can be defined in contrast to the bad anybody has necessarily also the potential to express. By definition, if I am good, I also can be bad, a necessary logical inference. Inversely, but more difficult to digest, the bad expressed in a person *only* exists and can be defined in contrast to the good this particular person has necessarily also the potential to express.

Empathy, a "good" force that brings individuals together, exists in contradistinction to the potential of its inverse, that is, social exclusion and rejection. Empathy and its inverse co-exist as potentials in all of us, with no exception. These opposite forces are selectively recruited depending on people and situations, whether it is to protect our progenies or strike enemies that threaten them. These forces are primarily regulated by three basic rules: (1) *in-group favoritism* (i.e., parochialism); (2) *the basic need to affiliate*; and (3) *the struggle for recognition* (reputation). These rules predict good as well as bad deeds. It also constrains us toward double standards and the compartmentalizing of our moral values, depending on people and situations. It is primarily what makes us the moral acrobats we are.

Serial killers do not hate everybody. They love their children, capable of being thoughtful and loving dads aside from being the pure monsters we see in them. No one is pure evil, except in our head. We are quick to hold the implicit clear-cut categorical assumption that monsters are just monsters, good people just good people. But such clear-cut assumptions are nothing more than convenient categorical anchorage giving traction to our moral decisions and justice distribution. They allow for the immediate creation of right

Moral Acrobatics. Philippe Rochat, Oxford University Press (2021). © Oxford University Press.
DOI: 10.1093/oso/9780190057657.003.0003

versus wrong values that reduce the whole picture of what a person is for quick judgments and decisions. Yet, those values depend on who is drawing judgments and making decisions: intimate friends, enemies, parents, just acquaintances, or the news media. In general, they depend on relative intimacy and proximal knowledge we entertain with the individual or group of individuals.

We have to recognize that serial killers are never just the crimes they incarnate and the ground for our demonization and, ultimately, their dehumanizing. By analogy, actors changing roles, if they act well, never become the single incarnation of the personage they play. Unlike spectators who tend to forget about the actor and get lost in the character (if the play is good), actors never lose sight of themselves playing and the character they play. They work to avoid getting lost in one, to the expense of the other. As for spectators of a play, monsters and enemies are created in our heads, fostered by fears and often by irrepressible needs for justice distribution, retribution, and closure by revenge. They also exist for heuristic convenience, thinking the world in black and white to avoid the heavy psychological cost of moral ambiguity.

Truman Capote hints at this view in his detailed crime investigation of two murderers he accompanied from their arrest up to their execution.[1] He unveils complex individuals, full of contradictions, twisted and torn by life circumstances and other accidents, committing an atrocious crime that ultimately brought them to the gallows. Their crime was particularly heinous, killing and disseminating an all-American hard-working Kansas farmland family. The killers, two ex-convicts on parole, were not simply monsters but rather an exacerbated, albeit perverted, expression of what we all are: compartmentalized beings that we construe in our heads as monsters and demons. Conjuring our fears, we represent monstrous and demonic essence in them that stands for the threat they represent to us personally as well as for the circle of our intimates, first and foremost. We tend to dehumanize them in the same way that they dehumanized their innocent victims to commit their crime. The suspension of humanity goes both ways.

The natural inclination toward demonizing and dehumanizing reveals not only our weakness as moral agents, but also what enables us to engage in torture and blind group violence like wars and ethnic cleansing, while continuing to be nurturing parents to our offspring. It reveals our ability to

---

[1] Capote, T. (1966). *In cold blood*. New York, NY: Random House.

switch moral codes and juggle multiple standards depending on whether we provide to our children, protect our kin, or fight our enemies. Our ability to switch moral codes depending on people and situations is the most unsettling issue of moral psychology.

As we will see next, it can be the source of much conflicts and constant torments within and among ourselves, as individuals or group of individuals. How do good people reconcile with their violent outbursts? How do otherwise peaceful individuals reconcile with their participation in atrocious collective violence and ethnic cleansing? Those are major and enduring psychological questions, far from being resolved and too rarely considered as conceptual anchors for thinking about the foundations of moral psychology.

Morality construed in the normative, categorical context of a good versus bad dichotomy does not capture the essence of what it actually means to be a human moral agent. Too clear-cut normative and binary, it lacks psychological validity. Primarily because it does not account for the code-switching aspect of our moral agency, an aspect that is at the core of great works of literature, like Dostoyevsky's *Crime and Punishment*. Yet it is rarely considered by moral philosophers, much less by moral psychologists, aside maybe from clinicians dealing with psychopathy or clinical theorists in the Freudian psychoanalytical tradition.

In his 19th-century novel, Dostoyevsky conveys a psychologically much more relevant "polyphonic" view on morality. The main protagonist—Rodion Raskolnikov—is torn and caught in constant oscillation between the right and the wrong, the good and bad deed: killing an unscrupulous and seedy pawnbroker to eradicate the moral vermin but also to steal his money. It is more paradigmatic of how we function as moral agents, always balancing right and wrong, good or bad, always ready to rationalize and transgress whatever norm, be it the simple etiquette of getting in line at a bus stop, containing sexual urges on a date, acquiring ownership of property, or the inclination toward basic equity in sharing. Rodion Raskolnikov is the paradigmatic embodiment of who we are as moral agent and what we all have to deal with psychologically in our social existence, more or less prone to cheat and lie, more or less able and motivated to refrain from transgressing, more or less aware of transgressing when we do so. We are sometimes good tippers, and other times, bad tippers, differentially inclined to cut lines or hand back excess money received by mistake from the bank teller, even when we are aware that the bank teller will probably be penalized by his boss to reimburse out of her own pocket.

Again, a crucial aspect of morality is that our standards and decisions tend to fluctuate and switch depending on our degree of intimacy with others, the situations and the kind of people we are dealing with. The main moral rule, psychologically speaking, is the fact that our moral compass is instantly recalibrated depending on people and situations. We hold different standards in our moral decisions whether people are in-group (same family, same social class, same language, same party, etc.) or out-group (legal or illegal immigrants, foreigners, stranger to the family, different skin color or body weight, etc.). If we are moral, we are moral chameleons, masters at switching moral codes at the tip of our fingers, from polite to crass. This is a universal expression and core issue of what it means to be "moral." It is never black or white, always fluctuating. To talk about morality in static, absolute, norma-tive, and categorical terms is disconnected from the psychological reality of what it means to be moral.

From two to three years of age children learn the indispensable rules of social deception like table manners covering up their urge to eat, pretending to know when they don't know at school, and vice versa, pretending that they don't know to keep a secret for fear of punishment or to maintain trust and reputation with in-groups. From the time we enter schools, even prior through the admonition and parental reinforcement of white "polite" lies and the pretense of social etiquettes, we engage in deliberate cover up and social deceptions indispensable to navigate the social world. We start our ca-reer as moral code switchers early, wearing multiple hats and balancing in-compatible standards: lying to some while keeping promises to others.

This basic aspect of morality is brought to scandalous levels by some adults, who while high in power get caught and are publicly exposed, revealing years of deception and code switching. Bernard Madoff was both Nasdaq high pro-file, family provider of a lavish lifestyle, and the pyramid scammer of the cen-tury who depleted the savings of thousands. Other examples abound, like the ex-budget minister of France Jerôme Cahuzac who came to power in 2012 as the new French Rambo against tax evasion. While in office, the press discov-ered that Cahuzac was hiding a stash of his own money in secret Swiss bank accounts to evade taxes. Fighting impeachment, Bill Clinton looked straight into the public eyes: "I want to say one thing to the American people. . . . I did not have sexual relations with that woman, Miss Lewinsky."

The only redeeming possibility for these public figures is that they are victims of their own confabulation: self-deceiving, becoming oblivious to the fact that they are actually lying, akin to the self-deception of compulsive liars. Remember the disbelief of O. J. Simpson at his trial when he tried to put on the infamous dry-blood, shrunken leather glove worn by the presumed assassin of his wife Nicole. Examples abound in the declared rationale of convicted serial killers like Ted Bundy before being executed, the common bad faith of politicians covering their prejudicial actions, the costly and immensely consequential made-up theories and other political hoaxes like Saddam Hussein's weapons of mass destruction. Nothing much you can do against bad faith, confabulation, self-deception, and other fake news. Bad faith is the source of much social ill. Its realization triggers a sense of irrelevance and helplessness in all of us.

In short, duplicity, righteousness, lying, self-deception, bigotry, moral biases, form the dark side of our empathic and cooperative inclinations. Looking at the state of our world, still filled with wars and violence, it is hard to claim that we are finally reaching "the age of empathy," as some would claim.[2] We tend to overlook the fact that bright and dark sides always complement each other. They do not exist to the exclusion of the other. These sides co-exist, leaning on each other and co-defined as Ying is to Yang, in spite of all of our radical and eliminative categorical propensities. Empathy and cooperation exist in contrast to their inverse: duplicity, lies, and self-deception. Bright and dark aspects of human nature are de facto complementary rather than antithetical, mutually incompatible and eliminative as we typically tend to construe them. They always co-exist.

Bright and dark sides of our morals develop hand in hand, leaning on each other. Children in their development tell us that we cannot consider them separately. Quickly developing the capacity to infer mental states in others (i.e., so-called theories of mind) as well as increasing concerns for others (empathic feelings and perspective taking), children also develop in parallel a capacity to fake, conceal, pretend, and lie. Somehow in a necessary and inseparable way, duplicity and self-deception in children develop with prosocial and cooperative inclinations. Co-defined, these opposite aspects emerge jointly in human ontogeny. They are the two sides of the same moral coin. As children develop conscientiousness, they also develop the potential for darker deeds.

[2] De Waal, F. (2009). *The age of empathy: Nature's lessons for a kinder society*. New York, NY: Harmony Books; HH The Dalai Lama. (2011). *Beyond religion: Ethics for a whole world*. New York, NY: Houghton Mifflin; see also, as mentioned in an earlier footnote, the recent critique by Paul Bloom in *Against Empathy* (2016).

"Beware of too smiley faces" recommends the protective father to his child. This advice points to a social reality that is duplicitous rather than black or white, right or wrong, good or bad. In the moral domain, nothing stands at face value. Yet, and in spite of it all, we all have the ingrained and naive propensity to think the world in black and white. How to make sense of it?

4

Value Creation and Moral Comfort Zones

As humans, our social experience rests primarily on the fact that we are constantly judging, assessing, creating, and defending subjective values for ourselves, for others, and, most important, in negotiation with others. We try to agree, share, and convince others on the relative quality of things, often but not always measured in reference to objective cost–benefit calculations. In hindsight, we reflect on the value of our decisions, whether it was right or wrong, profitable or not profitable, judicious or not.

Creating such qualitative values for ourselves, agreeing and sharing these values with others, is mainly what we do in life. We create sensuous, pleasurable moments for self and others like cooking and eating together the same food, drinking the same wine at the same time. Communal eating is universal and part of all human rituals and collective shared sensuous celebrations. This is true in all cultures, from the beginning of human evolution as prehistorical evidence of human feasts abound, including ethnographies of small bands of hunter-gatherers thought to mimic the ways of our ancestors.

Much of what we do in life is indeed to create values for self and in negotiation with others. *Homo negotiates,* we are as part of being *Sapiens sapiens,* the "wise wise man" that ironically stands for our distinct self-conscious species. The negotiation of values is for the most part subjective, rarely associated with absolute "objective" truth value, resulting, for example, from a mathematical operation like $1 + 1 = 2$. If there is absolute truth in the value resulting from such an operation, its psychological meaning is up for grabs, above and beyond the mathematical and logical necessity that $1 + 1 = 2$, and not 2.001 or 1.9. In actuality, the true experiential meaning of value resulting from such a necessary operation always remains negotiable and open-ended. Any objective result can have mundane or decisive existential relevance: adding one sugar cube because you take two in your tea or that both of your kids are back safe from school. The logical operation is invariant yet standing for incomparable content results. The content is always subjective in essence, requiring some negotiation and some sort of agreement with others—above

Moral Acrobatics. Philippe Rochat, Oxford University Press (2021). © Oxford University Press.
DOI: 10.1093/oso/9780190057657.003.0004

and beyond the logical necessity attached to the operation, which in itself is objective and absolute.

Fundamentally, we are compelled to share, agree, and create unity for ourselves but also *with* others. We synchronize our pains and pleasures by ways of compassion, sympathy, empathy, mimicry, or emotional contagion. We struggle for others' recognition and strive to create trust. We keep promises and make ourselves predictable to others, whether it is by telling the truth or by ways of deception. Value creation with others is indeed the main engine of social affiliation, the core lubricant of group fusion and of the contrast between "us" and "them." It is also our ways to create moral comfort for ourselves by making ourselves predictable and trustworthy to each other.

Our brain serves the main purpose of predicting what is going to happen next, in the physical and particularly in the social domain. We constantly gauge our present situation and factor experience in a similar past situation that we memorize and are familiar with. Like the brains of all animals or the software of any computer with learning capability, the human brain is primarily a guessing and future-predicting machine based on prior experience ("priors" in a Bayesian probabilistic jargon). But what makes the animal brain a very special guessing and gauging machine, unlike intelligent robots, is that it generates *feeling experience*.

A machine, by definition, does not feel or have emotions. It just thinks or processes information, sometimes better than the animal brain. It also does not have the irrepressible need to share. Thus, what is special about animal brains is that while processing information and learning to expect what is going to happen next, it is colored with feelings and emotions, the experiential or psychic "fume" emanating from its functioning as a biological information-processing machine. This psychic fume corresponds to the emotional or affective (phenomenal) awareness of being alive in that body, at this particular juncture in time. It stands for our subjective embodied experience, the experience of elation, attraction or repulsion, the good and not so good feelings we are able to experience in all things encountered in the here and now of our presence in the world. We cultivate this subjective experience for ourselves, but also most important for sharing and cultivating with others. The "coloring" experience of our affects is indeed our main social-exchange commodity, the stuff of our cooperation, from helping each other resolve problems or enterprising with others, gossiping, mourning, worshiping, or celebrating together.

Human subjective experience stands also for the good or not so good feelings we experience as we reminisce about the past or project into the future. It also stands for all the ambitions, desires, resentments, fears, guilt, shame, or pride that animates us and gives our life its ultimate value, its *existential worth* that ultimately defines our moral zones of comfort or discomfort, for ourselves as well as in negotiation with others.

Never just cold thinking machines, we create subjective values for ourselves and, more important, in negotiation with "others in mind."[1] Like any other living animals, we are first and foremost affective and emotional entities. Yet as humans and unlike other animals, we are also fundamentally moral and self-conscious, led by a unique and uncanny preoccupation of our own worth in relation to others: our reputation, moral stance, and identity, in general how we are perceived through the evaluative eyes of others.

The human brain generates a very unique kind of feeling experience, unlike any other animal brain. This experience is characteristically self-conscious and co-conscious with *others in mind.*[2] It is a feeling experience that is tainted by a particular kind of awareness regarding our own finitude, our own inescapable death to come in terms of absolute separation from those we know and are attached to, and the world on which we depend to survive. It is fundamentally the awareness of our own embodied and knowingly mortal self, as well as all the other knowingly mortal others.

Religious thoughts apart, the fact that we know we are going to die makes us a very different kind of evaluative creature, one that can project into the future with an absolute end point in sight. We are also unique creatures for dwelling into our past in search of identity in relation to others, reconstructing genealogical roots and building narratives about our origins. We can contemplate and try to fathom what happened prior to our birth and what will happen after we die. It is in the midst of such developing existential awareness and feeling experience that we strive to create value for ourselves and shared with others. This is true from the very beginning of life. Neonates strive to create value for themselves, reducing all kinds of stress (physical exhaustion, hunger, pain) via feeding, administrated cares like rocking, singing or caressing. They do create zones of calm and comfort for themselves, mainly though the attentive care of others (i.e., *comfort zones*) that by six weeks, with the emergence of socially elicited smiling,[3] they instinctively

---

[1] See Rochat, P. (2009). *Others in mind.* Cambridge, England: Cambridge University Press.
[2] That is the core argument made in a previous book (Rochat, 2009).
[3] See Rochat, P. (2004). *The infant's world* (Rev. ed.). Cambridge, MA: Harvard University Press.

want to share in primary, face-to-face intersubjectivity (the sharing of experience with others).

From the beginning of life, comfort zones are constructed around particular expected outcomes: food, faces, smells, voices, particular affective exchanges with others. We are indeed born in a world of values. Like any other living things, from the outset we are pushed and pulled by particular features in our environment: certain sounds; certain tastes, smells, or sights; certain people. Our own particular comfort zones are thus, at the origin, calibrated by certain affective experiences that we try to reproduce or avoid: things that we prefer over those we try to cancel or avoid. It provides primordial guidance to behavior as well as to its development.

Numerous empirical works demonstrate the importance of early experience in shaping preferences and attractions as opposed to avoidances or repulsions. For example, two-month-old infants are more attuned and prefer strangers whose interactive style in face-to-face interaction match the style of their own mother. If the mother tends not to be very responsive, they prefer less responsive strangers, and vice versa.[4] They quickly calibrate their interpersonal comfort zone based on past intersubjective exchanges with their mother as primary caretaker. Rat pups exposed to citrus scent put around the nipple of their dam will later prefer to mate with females whose sex smells like lemons. Sexually mature male rats are significantly more inclined to mount females that remind them of their first suckling experience as pups.[5]

At a shorter predictive time-scale, newborn infants prefer the smell of their own mother's amniotic fluid over the smell of another mother's liquid. They tend to orient significantly less toward the latter.[6] Quickly, infants start to discriminate their mother's *familiar* face over the face of another female stranger. From the outset, familiarity is key to value creation and early interpersonal comfort zones, in particular the selective attraction to people. Already, by five to six months after birth, infants are more inclined to pay attention to a stranger speaking their mother's tongue (English) with no

[4] Bigelow, A. & Rochat, P. (2006). Two-month-old infants' sensitivity to social contingency in mother-infant and stranger–infant interaction. *Infancy*, *9*(3), 313–325.

[5] Fillion, T. J., & Blass, E. M. (1986). Infantile experience with suckling odors determines adult sexual behavior in male rats. *Science*, *231*, 729–731.

[6] Marlier, L., Schaal, B., & Soussignan, R. (1998). Neonatal responsiveness to the odor of amniotic and lacteal fluids: A test of perinatal chemosensory continuity. *Child Development*, *69*(3), 611–623; Marlier, L., Schaal, B., & Soussignan, R. (1998b). Bottle-fed neonates prefer an odor experienced in utero to an odor experienced postnatally in the feeding context. *Developmental Psychobiology*, *33*, 133–145.

French accent.[7] Within weeks, infants create and are pulled toward the familiar. They are selectively attentive, weary, and quickly becoming fearful of the unfamiliar. The fact that from birth, and even prior to birth, the unfamiliar is source of puzzlement or surprise for the infant has been the single most important reliable phenomenon used by infancy researchers to unveil the secret of the young budding mind.[8]

From the beginning of life, thus, all we do is create values and comfort zones for ourselves that we quickly try to share and co-construct with others, always moving away from tensions and stress. If this inclination starts at birth, within months it is expressed with incommensurate degrees of symbolic complexity. As an adult, when I talk or write to you, I intend for you to understand what I am saying. I will talk until some agreement is reached. If we argue, we typically try to find some agreement and, hence, alleviate stress, social unease, and possibly costly fights. Value creation and agreement with others create the central core of social life. It is the main feature of how we manage to co-exist and somehow tame that selfish beast lying at rest in all of us. We know how to create comfort zones with selected others, which can quickly turn into affective cliques, the exclusive social bubbles where comfort zones are shared. The central question is, Why and who are those selected to share comfort zones? Who are those accepted within a particular exclusive bubble? Inversely, who are those who are rejected? Those are perennial psychological questions that need to be addressed if we want to understand our morals, in particular, our moral acrobatics.

Around the world, people tend to join forces and cooperate to further enhance values they share, practicing the same sport, eating together, rooting for the same team, reading the same literature, listening to the same music, or fighting for the same cause. Universally, we strive toward the co-construction of shared *comfort zones*, what we might refer to as harmonious co-existence with some, possibly the largest possible number of people, yet always by the necessary exclusion of others—those subjectively deemed incapable or not willing to share with the in-group.

In some instances, co-construction is replaced by coercion and other insistent attempts at conversion, from crusaders knocking on your door to ethnic cleansings and other religious massacres. The list is long, but always

---

[7] Kinzler, K. D., Dupoux, E., & Spelke, E. S. (2007). The native language of social cognition. *Proceedings of the National Academy of Sciences of the United States of America, 104*(30), 12577–12580.
[8] For a review, see Rochat, P. (2004). *The infant's world* (2nd ed.). Cambridge, MA: Harvard University Press.

expressing the same drive toward value creation around shared comfort zones, always linked to a process of exclusion of selected strangers. Shared comfort zones are buffers against what's unpredictable and unfamiliar. It is a buffer against what is strange or "barbarian" (i.e., unfamiliar strangers). It is a buffer against those who do not share the same etiquette and, as a consequence, are construed as a threat to one's group cohesion and harmony; those who do not share the same manners, the same taste for food, music, the same humor, the same verbal and gestural language, who do not carry their body and manage their self-presentation in the same way.

Shared comfort zones as normative attractors are elusive and subjective at best, yet both are experienced and represented in our heads as absolute, real categories that once learned and shared are hard to shake. The combination of value creation and the subjective experience and maintenance of comfort zones is a characteristic phenomenon of all groups, large or small. It exists in all cultures, and it is where one should look for the origin of our double standards, our categorical thinking of the world in black and white, our variable moral compass calibrated relative to social alliances and their respective shared zones of comfort. Criteria of social inclusion and exclusion, what is acceptable or not, right or wrong, vary across alliances and comfort zones. They are adjusted to the particular zone we experience as we navigate through our various alliance circles (spherical alliances discussed in a later chapter) of intimates, the immediate family circle, school, work team, army brigade, battalion, party, national citizenship. At each scale corresponds the experience of a different comfort zone. Various normative criteria apply for each with variable degrees of tolerance and consequences in case of a norm transgression. Across zones, there are different criteria of inclusion versus exclusion, different criteria of what is right versus wrong, what is normatively permissible or not, all with various consequences for the transgressor. Furthermore, the degree of individuals' commitment to group norms may vary across alliances and their respective comfort zone. Killing an anonymous passerby does not have the same normative weight compared to a parricide, even if (for argument's sake) in both cases the intent of the killer was to rob the same quantity of valuables. This relative normative commitment as a function of alliance and comfort zone is, I would assume, a universal truth, regardless of culture.

"Guest" or in-group, as a concept, exists and makes sense because it implies the existence of "nonguests" or out-group, people who are not invited to whatever party. It always implies unwelcoming and exclusion, setting criteria for who is in and who is out. The exclusion principle is always behind any so-cial clustering or categorization. Families, teams, tribes, gender, citizenship, ethnicities, and all the possible social categorizations refer to inclusion/ex-clusion criteria, from surface proxies like uniform, sex, skin color, ancestry, or passport from which we are universally inclined to infer and associate es-sential characteristics, often remarkably elusive and arbitrary. These essential properties of individuals or groups include merits, the potential for success and educability, intellectual aptitudes as in the case of the strong gender ster-eotype related to mathematics or spatial understanding (i.e., the so-called and well documented stereotype threat suffered by women who are consid-ered by default as less apt at math or finding their way in the environment).

We build our representations of the social world by clustering it on the basis of simple inferences and shortcut heuristics. We cannot help but falling prey to social stereotypes as they unquestionably facilitate our social navi-gation and our decision of what's right or what's wrong. They exist because they relieve us from painstaking self-reflective rumination in our value cre-ation. Stereotypes are filters simplifying our moral decisions. This is why we evolved and use such filters, in the moral domain, but also in all domains of brain functioning. This is mainly how our mind works: shortcutting and cat-egorizing for the sake of streamlining our thoughts, avoiding costly energy in rumination and time-consuming decision-making.

It is in reference to this general human context that we need to consider the nature of our moral decisions and human moral psychology in general. Next, I want to argue that being immoral is never equal to being devoid of morality. Claiming immorality in some individuals or group of individuals, including the most prototypical psychopaths like Hitler, Charles Manson, Ted Bundy, or Ahmad Rahami is essentially pointing to different morals compared to those recognized in one's own comfort zones. We are all moral, norm sen-sitive, and norm abiders, because we are endowed as a species with a psy-chology that is distinctively self-reflective and self-conscious. We express and live by different norms, different morals, each varying depending on the various comfort zones we navigate and in which we create zone-specific values: the value of intimacy, love and care in the intimate circle of family, friends and pets; the value of self-sacrifice and solidarity with nonbiological kin on the battlefield; obedience to authority at work, commanding authority as the leader of a group.

Even Hitler, the epitome of evil, the incarnation of bad and mad, happened also to be a vegetarian, with strong normative views on nature. He loved his pet and was not just devoid of morals. He created and abided to strong normative moral values created within his own exclusive comfort zones. As difficult as it might be, we are not different from Hitler in our moral functioning. Hitler built his own social views on the same premise as ours: using shortcuts, stereotyping, and clustering the world in black and white contrasts. What is different to most, and thankfully so, is the kind of values he created in his own circumstances. Hitler's extreme values and rigid morals illuminate important aspects of how we function in the moral domain, specifically how we manage to create values specific to our various existential comfort zones. Because Hitler in the Zeitgeist of the past six decades represents the normative incarnation of evil, he is a striking and memorable example of moral acrobatics.

Again, we build reputation around the values we create. They become part of our social identity and this identity always includes morals: a person's standards of thoughts, beliefs, and behavior. We always end up protecting and abiding to the value we create, as part of our self-reflective care for reputation. As such, we all end up with some sort of *morals*, values that are predictable of our person and an intrinsic part of who we are. As self-conscious entities, we all have morals. In sum, the question is not whether some have morals and others don't. The real questions are, What kind of morals, what are they made of, where do they come from, and, more important for this book, what holds them together in spite of blatant inconsistencies?

5

Hitler Was a Vegetarian

Hitler was contemptuous of meat eaters, a self-proclaimed vegetarian and militant protector of animals. At a romantic dinner date, he reportedly told a woman ordering sausage: "Go ahead and have it, but I don't understand why you want it. I didn't think you wanted to devour a corpse . . . the flesh of dead animals. Cadavers!"[1]

As he came to power in 1933, he and Nazi acolytes swiftly decreed strict animal protection laws preventing unnecessary cruelty and limiting the use of animals in medical research, ruling on the humane ways of butchering pigs, sheep, or birds. Nazis worshiped Nature, viewing animals above people, above non-Aryan people in particular. For example, a law prevented Jews to own pets. Whenever found, Jews' pets had to be gently anesthetized to prevent pain. The Nazi animal protection laws ruled against animal experimentation and Halal butchering. It advocated for the use of anesthesia before clipping dogs' ears, notwithstanding consideration regarding the cruel treatment of boiled lobsters. Hal Herzog pointedly comments in a recent special issue on animal ethics:

> We can learn a few things from the Nazis' stated concern for animal welfare. . . . The existence of a culture in which the leaders obsessed over the suffering of lobsters in Berlin restaurants while they were gassing people in concentration camps with rat poison represents a moral inversion of incomprehensible proportions. . . . The Nazi animal protectionists represent examples of fundamentally bad people doing good things for animals. I suspect this pattern of behavior is rare. However, the converse—fundamentally good people who treat animals badly—is common. In the United States, for instance, over 150 million animals are killed or wounded each year for the enjoyment of recreational hunters. Similarly, most childhood animal cruelty is perpetuated by children who will grow up to be perfectly normal adults. (The widespread belief that most school shooters and serial killers

---

[1] Waite, R. (1977). *The psychopathic god.* New York, NY: Basic Books, p. 19.

Moral Acrobatics. Philippe Rochat, Oxford University Press (2021). © Oxford University Press.
DOI: 10.1093/oso/9780190057657.003.0005

were early animal abusers is a myth.) Then there are the 10 billion animals slaughtered each year in the United States by what the philosopher Tom Regan calls "the tyranny of the fork."[2]

Regarding hunting, Hitler once commented: "I can't see what there is in shooting, you go out armed with a highly perfected modern weapon and without risk to yourself, kill a defenseless animal."[3]

At the end of war, at great risks, Hitler took his dog Blondi for walks outside the Berliner bunker under the Allied relentless bombing attacks. On April 30, 1945, Hitler died of a self-inflicted gun wound, his dog the day before swallowed a cyanide pill mixed with its daily food ration. Before committing suicide, Hitler was reportedly inconsolable of Blondi's death.

Hitler was also a devoted son, devastated when his mother died. His artistic ambitions led him to soup kitchens, homelessness, and a bohemian life for a few years, wandering the streets of Vienna, sleeping on park benches, and panhandling before he joined in 1914 the Bavarian army, which was part the German empire force during World War I (1914–1918). This enlistment was a source of renewed patriotism and heroic group exaltation. It became also the source of great national resentment following defeat and the humiliation of the 1919 Versailles peace treaty amputating Germany of 13% of its territories, including all colonies.

Forced to sign the treaty, Germany relinquished power over one ninth of its original population, contracting a huge reparation debt that did not help in its reconstruction. Combined with fears of a Russian Bolshevik revolution spilling over starting in 1917, the humiliating Versailles treaty contributed to the rapid Nazi effervescence and "chemical" precipitation that mobilized the majority of German people and all its industry in record time.

Reading Hitler's 1925 autobiography *Mein Kampf*, it appears that Nazi ideology and foreign policy find roots mainly in the deep resentment of Versailles, giving a rallying pretext and main traction to the Nazi party. From 1936, *Mein Kampf* becomes the German state's gift to all newlywed couples, like the "little red book" of Mao Zedong during the Chinese cultural

[2] Herzog, H. (2011, November 17). Was Hitler a vegetarian? The Nazi animal protection movement: What can we learn from Hitler's love of animals? *Psychology Today*. Retrieved from https://www.psychologytoday.com/us/blog/animals-and-us/201111/was-hitler-vegetarian-the-nazi-animal-protection-movement?amp=.

[3] Toland (1976, pp. 424–425); cited by Arluke, A. & Sax, B. (1992). Understanding Nazi animal protection and the Holocaust. *Athrozoos*, 5(1), 6–31.

revolution. Only 20 years later, Germany was ready to take the world, promoting pan-Germanism and Aryan purity way beyond its original frontiers.

Hitler as struggling, homeless, panhandling artist does not fit well with Nazi mass parades, particularly under the impeccable lens of Leni Riefenstahl's propaganda movies. In his teens, determined to become a visual artist, young Hitler flunked twice his admission examination to Vienna's art school, in 1907 and in the following year. What would have happened to the world had he been admitted? Possibly a more peaceful world, as only six years after coming to power, Hitler was leading and managed with the unconditional devotion of transfixed followers to put in place the totalitarian terror machine we know, sending millions to their death, in the most systematic (industrial) and sadistic genocidal ways in recorded history. Nazi apparatchiks repeat Hitler's moral acrobatics, from absolute genocidal propensities to animal empathy, as illustrated in the rather uncanny images below of Hitler engaged in affectionate petting (Figure 5.1).

Often tagged "criminal of the century," Gestapo-in-chief Heinrich Himmler was responsible for running all Nazi concentration and extermination camps. He was also a diehard vegetarian, fervently opposed to hunting. Here is what he reportedly volunteered to his doctor:

Figure 5.1 Hitler petting Blondi and a fawn.

How can you find pleasure, Herr Kerstein, in shooting from behind cover at poor creatures browsing on the edge of a wood—innocent, defenseless, unsuspecting? It's really pure murder. Nature is so marvelously beautiful and every animal has a right to live. It is this point of view that I admire so much in our forefathers. They, for instance, formally declared war on rats and mice, which were required to stop their depredations and leave a fixed area within a definite time limit, before a war on annihilation was begun against them. You will find this respect for animals in all Indo-Germanic peoples. It was of extraordinary interest to me to hear recently that even today Buddhist monks, when they pass through a wood in the evening, carry a bell with them, to make any woodland animals they might meet flee away, so that no harm will come to them. But with us every slug is trampled on, every worm destroyed.[4]

Hitler and his followers attributed much of Western civilization's decay to meat-eating, a source of impurity and crass vulgarity, notwithstanding insensitivity toward Nature and a general *lack of empathy*. They followed the steps of composer Richard Wagner whose grand music and lyrics they strongly admired and identified with. Wagner was indeed a strong advocate of vegetarianism, although Wagner could not strictly abide to it for health reasons. The Nazi party number-two man, Hermann Goering, was a formidable art collector and art aficionado. In Nazi ideology, Wagner's *Ring* represented the undisputed lyrical exaltation and aesthetic template of Aryan virtues. This artistic template was inseparable from a worship of Nature's force and beauty, from which derived the humane treatment of animals and, ultimately, Wagner's art and inspiration, as evidenced by a letter he wrote in 1858 to Mathilde Wesendonck, a German poet and close friend (b. 1828–d. 1902):

Recently, while I was in the street, my eye was caught by a poulterer's shop; I stared unthinkingly at his piled-up wares, neatly and appetizingly laid out, when I became aware of a man at the side busily plucking a hen, while another man was just putting his hand in a cage, where he seized a live hen and tore its head off. The hideous scream of the animal, and the pitiful weaker sounds of compliance that it made while being overpowered transfixed my soul with horror. Ever since then I have been unable to rid myself of this impression, although I had experienced it often before. It is dreadful to see

[4] Wykes, A. (1972). *Himmler*. New York, NY: Ballantine, pp. 89–90.

how our lives—which, on the whole, remain addicted to pleasure—rest upon such a bottomless pit of the cruelest misery! This has been so self-evident to me from the very beginning and has become even more central to my thinking as my sensibility has increased. . . . I have observed the way in which I am drawn in the (direction of empathy for misery) with a force that inspires me with sympathy, and that everything touches me deeply only insofar as it arouses fellow-feeling in me, i.e. fellow-suffering. I see in this fellow-suffering the most salient feature of my moral being, and presumably it is this that is the well-spring of my art.[5]

The offspring of Wagner's fellow-suffering moral being is also the fellow-killing morality of what became the Nazi party. Incongruous? Not really, if we scratch the surface and move beyond our gut, dumbfounded reaction. In today's Western middle class, industrialized, and rich context, we tend to associate the refusal to eat meat with concerns for animal welfare and nature in general, not just with potential health issues. As mentioned earlier, being a vegetarian is typically perceived and presented as a political, ecological, if not religious life decision with the implicit blanket statement of disgust and refusal to kill. In such Western middle-class context, who would have thought that Nazism and vegetarianism were compatible?

In fact, such dumbfounded reaction to Nazi promotion of vegetarianism and antihunting sentiments reflects on the radical, dualistic, essentialist, and basically compartmentalized views we tend to have regarding morality. The fact that most of us experience such incongruity reveals the narrow nature and rigid aspect of our fundamentally dichotomous moral and demonizing stance: either good or bad, never good *and* bad, as expressed not only in Hitler's aversion to animal cruelty, but also the serial killers' love for their children or the current Buddhist violence against Muslims taking place in Myanmar. Such brutal violence from a religious group preaching equanimity and vegetarianism is in many ways homologous to Nazi politics of evacuation and systematic elimination against the Jews, Gypsies, and homosexuals. Incongruous it is, but only on the surface and for those who do not dwell in cultural history and other social anthropological theories, which actually make sense of such immediate incongruity.

[5] Wagner, R. (1987). *Selected letters of Richard Wagner* (S. Spencer & B. Millington, eds. and trans.). New York, NY: Norton.

There are historical reasons why Nazism accompanied the edict of humane laws toward animals placed above some human groups like the Jews. Like any totalitarian and genocidal regime, Nazi ideology was obsessed with in-group Aryan purity, obsessed with the cleansing of impure elements, a pattern universally described in tribal and other ethnic massacres from Cambodia, Rwanda, and Serbia to current conflicts in Syria, Yemen, Ukraine, or Myanmar. It is universal that strong, totalitarian in-group affiliation is commensurate to the fear of contamination from both without and within. The frenzy of eliminating parasitic out-group members always correlates with an obsession in the detection of in-group impure traitors (interior enemies) constantly in need of being "purged."

These kinds of purges were most evident, for example, during the terror era of the French Revolution, when leaders were sent to the guillotine as enemies of the republic as quickly as they were elected to power by the people's assembly. The pure/impure opposition with typical use of bodily and biological metaphors is universal in totalitarian regimes that typically qualify impure out-group and in-group (traitor) members as vermin, roaches, rats, dust, or viruses. Now the in-group/out-group dynamic of purification can have many different forms and expressions, depending on historical and cultural circumstances, existing myths and taboo, as well as economic realities that play a role in the expression of such dynamics. Enemies can be Jews, Bosnians, Tutsis, or Christians and the rationale for fights and purges adapted to the historical and cultural circumstances of the time. In the Nazi era, there was the pan-Germanism need to unify the in-group around a language and an identity, draw cultural lines, piggy backing on the neo romantic nostalgia expressed in Wagner's lyricism, century old anti-Semitic traditions, the humiliation of a defeat, communist threat, and an economic chaos—all multifactor ingredients for the Nazi recipe.

6

No Pure Monsters

On August 1, 2013, a Cleveland court sentenced Ariel Castro to life in prison plus 1,000 years, without parole. The condemnation was swift and unequivocal. Juan Perez, a young man who grew up in the neighborhood, tells news reporters upon learning of Castro's arrest:

> He was a nice guy, he would come around and say hi. He gave the kids rides up and down the street on his four-wheeler. . . . um, I've known him since I was like five or six years old myself he would asked me if I wanted a ride. . . . He seemed like he was a good guy to the kids that were here, I don't think he had any bad intentions with the kids that were on the block. . . . I didn't think anything of it. . . . He made himself out to be to the block, not shy to attend a backyard party or barbeque.[1]

Perez lived all his life a few houses from where Castro committed his abominable crimes. He was stunned and ashamed for not being even suspicious of what went on for years in the house next door.

Castro abducted and repeatedly raped three women in his house over an 11-year period. The three women were chained, fed one meager meal a day, and treated like sex slaves. The crime mesmerized people worldwide, and the American flag dangling on the porch of Castro's infamous Cleveland house shamed America.

In 2007, one of the women gave birth to a child, fathered by Castro. The child could have been fathered by some of his friends or one of his two brothers, regularly invited for some "parties" at the house. The crimes were of despicable cruelty and Castro's infamous house on Seymour Avenue became a symbol of horror reproduced on the front page of all tabloids. It was swiftly razed to erase memories.

---

[1] Berry, A., & DeJesus, G. (2015). *Hope: A memoir of survival in Cleveland.* New York, NY: Penguin Books; excerpt taken from *People Magazine* (2015, May 4), p. 64.

Moral Acrobatics. Philippe Rochat, Oxford University Press (2021). © Oxford University Press. DOI: 10.1093/oso/9780190057657.003.0006

Castro was a fervent Catholic, going to mass every Sunday at a local church, and was said to be affable and kind to generations of kids he drove back and forth from school as an official bus driver for 30 years. Often, neighbors saw Castro strolling with his youngest child to a nearby public park for some playground activities. During his short trial, he volunteered a 16-minute defense plea. "I am not a monster" was his opening line. With a soft, dispassionate voice, Castro depicts the love and family atmosphere that reigned at the house during the years of abduction, claiming that all the sex that happened during that time was consensual. For defense and to avoid a death sentence, he mentions being abused as a child and a long addiction to porn.

Two decades prior, serial killer Ted Bundy offered the same exact rationale for his acts. In an interview volunteered just hours before sitting on the electric chair for raping and killing over 30 Florida women, Bundy comes across handsome, sincere, and charming, the same way he appears in previous interviews. However, this time he is actually about to die. It is chilling. On September 3, 2013, barely two months into his life plus 1,000-year sentence, Ariel Castro took upon himself to take his own life. Escaping surveillance, he wrapped sheets around his neck and hung himself in his solitary cell.

Clinical psychologists would say that Ariel Castro and Ted Bundy are both textbook cases (here, deadly cases) of full-blown narcissistic personality disorder, utmost expressions of self-delusion. In fact, I would argue that they are much more than extreme cases of psychopathy. Like other mental illness amplifying what is latent in all of us typically functioning individuals, Castro and Bundy are extreme cases of the kind of balancing acts we all have to perform to survive as self-conscious moral agents, struggling for social recognition and caring for their reputation, surrounded by others as judges. Criminal or not, such balancing acts are what preserve our unity as individuals, our own sense of moral coherence without which we collapse psychologically, opening doors to the mayhem of madness and social isolation. What maintains self-unity is indeed the central issue of moral psychology, what keeps us together as individuals and as groups.

Who was Castro? Was he just the direct reflection of his monstrous crimes? Was he just reducible to his despicable acts? Close acquaintances of criminals, like Perez in relation to Castro, have typical difficulties in reconciling the person they knew with the crimes they are accused of: "How could he have done this?" "It is not possible," "You've got to have the wrong person." Again, such expressions of disbelief from neighbors and family members are a common, often integral part of the crime reports on local news. It is an object of public fascination, the bread and butter of tabloids trying to uncover truth.

Amanda Berry, the abducted woman who gave birth to Castro's child in captivity writes in a recent autobiography: "He kidnapped me, chained me like a dog, raped me over and over. But he was Jocelyn's father. She loves him and he loved her." Upon hearing the news of Castro's suicide in jail she writes: "Ariel Castro deserved to be in jail, forever. But now that he's suddenly dead, I don't know what to feel, and that confusion is running in rivers down my cheeks."[2]

***

In sum, and to conclude this first part of the book, we have to come to terms with the fact that terrorists and serial killers love their parents and children. They worship their God and, in most instances, show extreme devotion to others that can lead to horrendous self-sacrifices like suicide bombings. As much as they kill, they also reciprocate affections and dedication from family members, neighbors, or close ideological allies. Pure monsters do not exist, and this is difficult, if not impossible for us to either fathom or digest. High-ranking Nazis were often cultured. They had a coherent romantic cult of Nature and narrative regarding the cult of their own mythical origins as part of a "pure" Aryan species, a narrative powerful enough to rationalize the eradication of millions of "impure" individuals following strict and well-articulated fetishist blood lineage law. They also loved Mozart, had strong views on aesthetics, and many of them were accomplished musicians. Whether we like it or not, Nazis had "morals" and hence were not pure irrational monsters. They were also parents, children, and friends. If not pure monsters proper, they expressed a most extreme moral ambiguity and hypocrisy, a hideous exaggeration of what we actually all are. We have to own up to this if we want to grow wiser.

As we will try to articulate and discuss further in the next three sections of the book, we can try to make sense of such phenomenon, based on how the mind seems to work, not only from an adult perspective, but also from the perspective of child development. Research in this realm shows that infants from birth are categorical in their perceptions. From a very early age kids

---

[2] Berry, A., & DeJesus, G. (2015). *Hope: A memoir of survival in Cleveland.* London, England: Corgi Books; excerpt taken from *People Magazine* (2015, May 4, 2015), p. 64.

"essentialize" things, compelled to infer nonobvious essences into things: for example, a blanket is endowed with the power to reduce stress and separation anxiety.[3] These essences are the source of much self-delusion as well as delusion about others, the products of our own imagination. They are not real and do not exist in a physical sense. Like mental ghosts, they exist at a representational or symbolic level. Although not concrete physical entities, the power of these ghostly representations is unlimited, leading to great passions often deeply irrational and potentially devastating. We are creationists and fetishists by nature. This is part of our poisoned gift from nature as members of a self-conscious and symbolic species.

The bet proposed here is that owning up to our creationist and overly caricaturizing mind will help us gain some wisdom, the only way to mitigate our unlimited potential for violence. This violent potential is the perversion of protective and survival instincts we share with all other animals, but that we bring to new, incomparable self-conscious and symbolic levels.

We should never lose track of the fact that we are the only species reveling in revenge and retribution. We are the only species that tortures; exploits; ostracizes; and engages in ethnic purification, ideological crusades, and other imperialist conquests, in addition to being carnivores like many other creatures, eating meat and killing other animals. We are unique in our cultivation of war as "art," a perennial human source of affiliation and pleasure, elevating intraspecific conflicts as symbolic sources of honors, heroism, and enhanced individual as well as group reputation.

To become eventually wiser, we have primarily to own up to such uncanny potential, the apparent source of pleasure, comfort, and transcendence we seem to find in violence oriented to other fellow humans construed as enemies. A first step toward becoming wiser, eventually more tolerant and restrained in our potential to cause harm, would be to own up to the fact that such violent potential is always commensurate to all the good we are capable of toward our kin and neighbors. As a species, we bring the bad and the good to new, incomparable self-conscious and symbolic levels.

As much as we have an unmatched potential for violence, we also have an unmatched potential for social collaboration, sources of all the ratcheting new technologies, discoveries, and cultural transmissions, the stable consensual laws and all the myriads of collective constitutions that govern human

---

[3] Gelman, S. A., & Davidson, N. S. (2016). Young children's preference for unique owned objects. *Cognition, 155,* 146–154.

societies, from family, to villages, small businesses, large companies, states, and group of nations like NATO, the European Union, or the United Nations Organization.

Neither saints nor pure monsters, we grow value for ourselves and those we identify with, at all levels. This is not just a dark view of the human condition. It is an actual sign of health and well-being, the secret of our striving and survival as self-conscious animals. It also entails much of the moral ambiguities and hypocrisy discussed here, all seen as by-products of our essentialist, one-sided categorical view of what we construe as the "good life": understanding the world in black and white; good versus bad.

The human mind breathes obligatory dichotomies with a subjective sense of deep mutual exclusivity, all products of our imagination, the products of our self-conscious, self-protective, and essentialist mind making us the compartmentalized moral beings we are. Despite the little scrutiny it would take, we remain blind to and scared of the simple idea that the bright doesn't exist without the dark, and vice versa. Yet the latter is even more difficult for us to endorse and to internalize. It is indeed harder to conceive the bright side of dark individuals, than the reverse. It is difficult for us to accept that "even damnation is poisoned with rainbows."[4] This asymmetry is at the core of our moral judgments. Owning up to it makes us wiser.

---

[4] Cohen, L. (1969). "The Old Revolution" [Song]. In *Songs from a Room* [Album]. Nashville, TN: Columbia.

PART 2

PROCLIVITIES

What Guides Our Moral Decisions?

In the midst of such conundrum, basic predictable motives and proclivities drive our moral decisions. These include the way we tend to compartmentalize our alliances with others, our need for exclusivity, and our inclination toward parochialism which always to the detriment of some others. The next series of chapter deal with these proclivities, seen here as ultimately guiding our moral decisions, also accounting for our inescapable moral ambiguities.

7

Moral Sphere Collapses

"I'd like to thank my family for loving me and taking care of me, and the rest of the world can kiss my ass."[1] These are the last words of Johnny Garrett before being executed by lethal injection in Texas for the 1981 rape and murder of a 76-year-old nun. He was only 18 at the time of the crime, 28 when he died in 1992. These last words epitomize the cleavage between proximal in-group and distal out-group value systems and moral codes for which radically different moral standards apply. Extreme as it might be in this particular case, what Garrett's last words exemplify is what is universally experienced: the well-separated moral spheres we live in, specifically delimited by context and people. These spheres call for different moral biases and codes. They are typically well compartmentalized and we develop a remarkable ability to switch moral codes depending on people and circumstances, as exemplified by Hitler and his pet dog or Ariel Castro with his child and neighbors. However, collapse between these spheres may happen causing great anxieties, and in some instances, they can be lethal, as we will see. Moral code implosions due to such collapse are the main cause of guilt, a major conundrum of human psychology. It can have serious consequences in the life of both the individual and the group.

Françoise Sironi is a French clinical psychologist and co-founder of the Primo Levi Center (http://www.primolevi.org/), which focuses on the care of victims of torture and political violence. She specializes in the treatment of not only victims of torture, but also their torturers. Sironi[2] points to the fact that states that condone torture do not recruit particularly sadistic individuals to fabricate individual torturers.

Based on her long clinical experience with both victims of torture and torturers themselves from all over the world, she found no clear evidence of

---

[1] STATE OF TEXAS AGAINST GARRETT, reported, *APBnews.com* a former a criminal-justice-centered newsmagazine, *archived 2002-02-09, also* quoted in "The Last Word": A 2008 film by Jesse Quackenbush.

[2] Sironi, F. (2009). *Bourreaux et victimes: Psychologie de la torture* [Torturers and victims: Psychology of torture], Paris, France: Odile Jacob.

Moral Acrobatics. Philippe Rochat, Oxford University Press (2021). © Oxford University Press.
DOI: 10.1093/oso/9780190057657.003.0007

known psychopathology associated with torturers. She reports instead that those becoming torturers tend to have been victims themselves of dehumanizing and humiliation, often associated with a rough authoritarian education. What she reports is that all torturers are the products of the same systematic "de-empathizing" training program consistently put in place in states with torture techniques that are remarkably analogous across cultures and places. It is similar in many ways to the mind-breaking techniques found in army boot camps all over the world.

In her seminal 2009 book, Francoise Sironi demonstrates that the fabrication of torturers and their victims are in fact the result of the same basic dehumanizing and de-empathizing process. Victims of torture tend eventually to mirror the process that created the torture victims they are. For Sironi, both victims and their torturers are typically entrapped in the same dehumanizing process. Both require the same kind of posttraumatic treatments. Paradoxically, and this is the main message that Francoise Sironi conveys in her book, both torturers and victims have been reduced to the same silencing process of their humanness, creating a strange implicit alliance between the two.

At a Paris conference on torture in 2013 (*Un monde tortionnaire, lancement du rapport ACAT, action des chrétiens pour l'abolition de la torture* | www.acatfrance.fr) she gave a talk, "The Making of Torturers." In her talk,[3] Sironi retells the story of one of her patients, a Turkish torture victim. At the end of a torture day, another victim hangs beside him from the ceiling. Totally exhausted, he lashes out at his torturer who is ready to leave: "Are you done with your day now? Going home? Are you going to tell your wife and children what you just did to me?" In response, the torturer finished him up, torturing him to death before leaving the room.

This grim example typifies the fact that we live in different moral spheres, hermetically compartmentalized. As Sironi points out in her talk, the torturer could not reconcile the dehumanized and de-empathized code of the torture room with the humanized and empathic code outside the chamber. The two collapsed, and this implosion was lethal for the victim. A moral cleavage is necessary to avoid collapse. Such cleavage is also expressed by serial killers in relation to their children and close family members, as emphasized by Daniel Zagury,[4] a French psychiatrist who wrote extensively on the

---

[3] Sironi's talk can be heard on YouTube (https://www.youtube.com/watch?v=393TFPoVn7I).
[4] Zagury, D. (2008). *L'énigme des tueurs en série* [The enigma of serial killers]. Paris, France: Plon.

topic based on numerous in-depth psychiatric cases of individuals, who for the past few decades have been arrested in France and condemned for systematically killing multiple people. Moral codes flip-flop radically across these social spheres.

French novelist Romain Gary tells "the tale of the chameleon" in reference to his multicultural upbringing and life exposure:

> Lay the chameleon on a red carpet, it becomes red. Lay the chameleon on a green carpet, it becomes green, we placed it on a yellow carpet, it became yellow, we placed it on a blue carpet it became blue, and we put the chameleon on a multicolor Scottish tartan and the chameleon became insane.[5]

In a previous book,[6] I presented the example of a similar sphere and moral code collapse using of a fictive John, inspired by a clinical case reported to me some years ago. Clinical rather than criminal, the case is a good paradigm of collapsing spheres normally well compartmentalized. It is reproduced in the next chapter.

---

[5] Gary, R. (2014). *Le sens de ma vie—entretien* (meaning of my life—interview). Paris, France: Gallimard, NRF, p. 17. (French translation by the author)

[6] Rochat, P. (2009). *Others in mind*. New York, NY: Cambridge University Press.

8

A Heart Made of Abundance

John is a happily married man with two young children. But he has a few mistresses that he loves and enjoys.[1] Furthermore, from time to time, on his own and secretly, he takes pleasure trips to a large city nearby for wild nights in gay bars and other same sex public bath spots. Who is John? Which one of his various contexts captures best the essence of what he might be as a person? Is John as a person better captured by the role he plays as father? Husband? Lover? Or is it John the explorer of new pleasures? It appears that it is none of these roles taken separately as illustrated by one of John's dream.

One night, as John is sleeping in the conjugal bed, he woke up by his wife's side, breathing fast and heavily, soaked in cold sweat. He felt that he was dying, and so thought his wife, who never witness her husband in such deep panic state. Seizure was the first thing that came to her mind, ready to rush him to the hospital. The seizure turned out to be a violent reaction to a nightmare that drove John into absolute panic. Here is John's horrendous dream:

> As a good son, he took his mother shopping. After a calm spree at some stores, he took her for a drink at a bar. The hostess welcoming them was his wife, the waiter was one of his male lovers, and when he went to the bathroom, he bumped into two of his mistresses that were chatting and giggling at the bar. All of the contexts of his life had coalesced into one.

John woke up in a cold sweat when, in his dream, he eventually stood frozen in the middle of the bar with all the eyes of the protagonists staring at him: mother, wife, mistresses and male lover. Under the crossfire of these gazes, John, in his dream, felt that his embodied person was melting. This is when he woke up in a panic. The multiple contexts of his affective life were collapsing and he was dying, his personhood vanishing.

---

[1] This chapter is taken verbatim from Rochat, P. (2009). *Others in mind*. Cambridge, England: Cambridge University Press, p. 204.

Moral Acrobatics. Philippe Rochat, Oxford University Press (2021). © Oxford University Press.
DOI: 10.1093/oso/9780190057657.003.0008

One could argue that John's dream is driven by guilt, that it is just a dream about being unmasked, a situation where well kept secrets are being brought to light, in this case compartmentalized relations running into one another. There is certainly an element of truth, but this interpretation eludes the fundamental question of John's experienced personal identity. In the dream, there is someone, i.e., John, who presumably experiences strong emotions, whether guilt, embarrassment, jealousy, love, and ultimately the panic fear that wakes him up. A first-person perspective is the prerequisite for the experience of guilt or any kind of emotions. So who is John in the end, as expressed in his dream?

John, in reality and in the dream, lives multiple lives that, apparently, are not incompatible. He managed to survive the juggling of relational involvements for years. In his case, there have been a few bumps and convoluted instances, but nothing out of the ordinary. One time, for example, he had unsafe sex with a man and worried that he could contaminate his female lovers. For a few weeks he had to make up stories to avoid sex with them until his HIV test came back negative. This was a constant worry in John's adventurous and risky love life, but other than that, nothing out of the ordinary for John.

His life was fulfilling and he was obviously not hurting any of those involved with him. For the most part, he was a decent husband who enjoyed being with his wife, a caring father and an intense lover in all his extramarital affairs. So what went wrong in his dream?

The life John manages is marked by tightly compartmentalized contexts that call for specific roles: the role of husband, the role of straight lover, gay lover, and father. All these roles are linked to different sets of values and emotions, a variety of intimate relations and relational domains or microcultures: the family culture, the culture of durable husband and wife relationship, the excitement of passing passions and the lust of momentary sexual encounters. Each context requires John to play a different role, assume different values, and change the pace and the intensity of his exchanges with the particular protagonist(s) crossing his intimate lives. This juggling of roles is possible only if each relational context is well delimited and confined, allowing for a smooth switching from one to another, with no interferences from any of them onto the other.

In the dream, the hermetic barrier separating each of John's contexts collapsed and his sense of person literally vanished, as in death. John's reaction to his nightmare was the virtual death of his personhood, I would suggest. In relation to the discussion of what is the self and what might constitute identity, we are still eluding the question of who is John, namely who is the person dying in his nightmare, what constitutes the notion of his personhood?

In my 2009 book I conjecture that in his juggling of roles, John is none of them in particular. He is not first and foremost a husband and a father who is going astray from normal family life. I argue that John is *all* the roles he created in his life, driven by circumstances, encounters, and propensities he carried within him (his sexual appetite for example). However, John, the way he experiences his personal identity and how his person is experienced by others, is not just the addition or average of all his social roles.

The essence of what John is, as a person, is what emerges from the process of *transition* from one role to another. John needs all the social contexts and the roles associated with each of them to approximate who he is conceptually. What John perceives and represents of himself as a person rests on the switching of all the social roles he plays. It is in the switching of roles that he gets some grip as to what he might be. John's identity is all the roles that compose his person, yet he is none, since what he is, is in between roles, revealed as he switches from one to another.

What caused John's horrendous nightmare would be the coalescence of all the intimate protagonists of his life brought in one single context. In his dream, I would argue, John lost touch with what he was as a person because the whole process through which he could experience his personhood was suddenly suspended. He lost the opportunity to control and experience the transition from one context to another, all collapsing into one in the dream, not anymore compartmentalized with him jumping from one to another at will. No more transition to be experienced, no more invariants specifying who he was as a person. The source of panic and terror comes from the fact that in the dream John is vanishing, literally dying as he loses the means to reveal himself as a person in the *process* of transiting from role to role. Personhood, and in particular the self as moral agent, is indeed a social process, not a static thing. There is no objective moral agent in itself, just as there is no cloud in itself: there is just something revealed in transition. The self as moral agent is revealed in transition from code to code, sphere to sphere, like the cloud is revealed by the constant transition of air masses from gas to solid state.

9

Spherical Alliances

Another way to construe the sphere collapse and "role implosion" of John (see preceding chapter) is to look beyond his particular individual subjective experience and see it from the point of view of John's relation to others, across the various contexts in which he performs his roles as father, son, husband, or lover. Aside from dictating a specific role to John, each context is also associated with a particular connection, a dominant affective component like love, care, duty, or authority linking John to the various protagonists within a particular contextual sphere: mother, children, wife, lovers, co-workers, boss, or employees. In addition, within each sphere, social and affective connections stand at different stages of their respective interpersonal development or evolution. There is indeed a lot to juggle in anybody's life, even if it is not as eccentric and adventurous as in the case of fictive John.

The particular affective connection within a contextual sphere resembles what therapists call *alliance* when talking about what links them to a patient, an important concept that, in fact, captures the affective core of any social relationship. A therapeutic alliance is operationally defined in terms of tasks, goals, and bond.[1] The task is what protagonists agree upon as to what needs to be done within the contextual sphere. The goal is what protagonists expect to gain within the contextual sphere. And finally, the bond is the mutual trust that links the protagonists within a sphere.

In general, for each of our contextual spheres there corresponds a particular "working" alliance, defined by specific functional task, goal, and bond. For example, in John's familial sphere, the main task is to support and provide for his children, the goal is to prepare them for life, and the bond is the trust that all protagonists will do their best in their respective roles within the sphere.

John's alliances to mother, wife, or lovers are specific and not collapsible, each referring to their respective contextual sphere. These alliances are

---

[1] See Bordin, E. S. (1979). The generalizability of the psychoanalytic concept of the working alliance. *Psychotherapy: Theory, Research & Practice, 16*(3), 252–260.

Moral Acrobatics. Philippe Rochat, Oxford University Press (2021). © Oxford University Press.
DOI: 10.1093/oso/9780190057657.003.0009

compartmentalized and specific. John remains the same person but wears different responsibilities or alliance hats across contextual spheres. Each sphere has its unique line-up of protagonists and demands. If you go along with this picture of John, the question is, How does he manage to bind all of these spheres and corresponding alliances in his head as obviously *he* (and nobody else) navigates between them? In his navigation, as he changes hat, he certainly does not become somebody else each time. Like a good actor, and contrary to individuals suffering from multiple-personality disorders, John never loses himself totally in his current "spherical" role. His case just exemplifies how far one can push the limits of natural roleplaying, an exploration that can lead to much anxiety and guilt, as expressed in the recurrent nightmares leading John to seek therapeutic help.

In instances of dissociative identity disorder (DID), and unlike the case of John, according to the most recent *Diagnostic and Statistical Manual of Mental Disorders* (DSM-5),[2] individuals suffering from DID experience distinct personality states, each marked by compartmentalized and deep differences in affect, cognition, perception, memory, sensory-motor functioning, and, ultimately, experienced identity. DID diagnosis includes experiences of possession as it is observed in certain religious rituals and have been documented by pioneer visual anthropologist Jean Rouch in his classic 1955 *Les Maîtres Fous* (*The Mad Masters*; available on YouTube).

In general, there are two competing models accounting for what might cause DID-related phenomena that all scientists acknowledge are not just pseudo or fake phenomena.

One model (the posttraumatic model) construes DID as expression of coping mechanisms triggered by violent traumas that lead victims to dissociate and compartmentalize their personality into discrete "alters" or alter egos. By analogy, it is not unlike the mental escape route victims of torture report taking by impersonating someone else, extracting themselves from the present situation by fitting into another personality and role. As philosopher Daniel Dennett writes in relation to multiple-personality disorder and its link to childhood trauma: "[Victims of trauma] manage to preserve themselves by redrawing of their boundaries. What they do, when confronted with overwhelming conflict and pain, is this: they 'leave.' They create a boundary that the horror doesn't happen to them: it either happens to no one, or to

---

[2] American Psychiatric Association. (2013). *Diagnostic and Statistical Manual of Mental Disorders* (5th ed.). Arlington, VA: Author.

some other self."[3] Indeed, a lot of patients diagnosed with DID report being abused as a child and other intense childhood traumas such as rape.

Yet another model of dissociative identity disorder proposes a more social and cognitive account of DID.[4] According to this model, DID would be more like a "fad diagnosis" as portrayed in popular films like the blockbuster *Sybil* and induced in the patients by the therapist. The diagnosis would be socioculturally constructed, more or less created by the therapist (so-called iatrogenic) rather than a symptom endogenous to patients as a direct result of particular trauma or life history:

> As the idea of multiple personality pervades our popular culture, suggestible people coping with a chaotic current life and a severely traumatic past express discomfort and avoid responsibility by uncovering "hidden personalities" and giving each of them a voice. This is especially likely when there is a zealous therapist who finds multiple personality a fascinating topic of discussion and exploration.[5]

Psychopathology aside, we all navigate through multiple social spheres, staging ourselves and adopting various roles depending on circumstances dictating particular alliances, as in the extreme case of John whose incompatible social spheres collapse, imploding in the recurrent narrative of his dreams, presumably under the weight of guilt and the psychic pressure of keeping them tightly compartmentalized.

The alliance within a sphere represents an interpersonal moral norm of trust and expectations: the sphere of John and his wife, John and his children, John and his lovers, and John and his mother, each with their own stories and specific evolution with particular affective events loading each sphere with its own memories. Transgression within a sphere is relative to the particular norm of the "spherical" alliance. Treasons, secrets, and confessions are always relative to such interpersonal norms. These norms represent a well compartmentalized relational or interpersonal value system. Hitler had a particular alliance with his dog Blondi; Ariel Castro, with his daughter, mother, and

---

[3] Dennet, D. (1991). *Consciousness explained.* Boston, MA: Little Book, p. 150.

[4] See Spanos, N. P., Weekes, J. R., & Bertrand, L. D. (1985). Multiple personality: A social psychological perspective. *Journal of Abnormal Psychology, 94*(3), 362–376.

[5] Fances, A., & First, M. B. (1998). *Your mental health: A layman's guide to the psychiatrist bible.* New York, NY: Scribner, pp. 286–287, cited in Lilienfeld, S. O., & Lynn, S. J. (2015). *Dissociative identity disorder: A contemporary scientific perspective.* In S. O. Lilienfeld, S. J. Lynn, & J. M. Lohr (Eds.), *Science and pseudoscience in clinical psychology* (2nd ed., pp. 113–152). New York, NY: Guilford Press.

fellow parishioners; the torturer, with his wife and kids. These spherical alliances are moral ecosystems that are typically well compartmentalized but can permeate and collapse as in the case of John or the deadly snapping of the Turkish torturer related by Françoise Sironi. These moral ecosystems exist in parallel to the pervert alliances linking torturer and victim. Across spheres, radically different standards and moral norms may apply, a central feature of moral psychology that is too often overlooked and played down by researchers. It is at the core of this book.

If we acknowledge the reality of moral spheres, then the question is, How do individuals juggle them? How do we manage to reconcile these spheres, each with their normative and affective specificity without losing the sense of our personal and interpersonal unity? How can a guy like Castro be affectionate with his mother after raping one of his victims, take his child to church after treating the mother as a sex slave, looking at her in the eyes, showing love and tenderness, switching modes with not much blinking. How does one manage to keep self-unity as moral agent while enacting blatant moral disconnects across alliances, something we all do to some degree, not just psychopaths? Where is our moral self-unity and what does it say about moral psychology in general?

To start addressing this question, we should consider first what underlies human proclivities to create and maintain alliances that are by definition exclusive. We all share evolved proclivities by which we instinctively create exclusivity, an "exclusivity instinct" as discussed in the next chapter. Such proclivities provide some common ground and a starting point to think about psychological unity in the midst of all our moral acrobatics.

10

Exclusivity Instinct

We are so constituted that we can gain intense pleasure only from
the contrast, and only very little from the condition itself.
—Sigmund Freud, *Civilization and Its Discontents*

Meaning creation is based on categorization: parsing and the creation of a
conceptual gist about things. The way we make sense of the world depends
on such a process. The main function of the mind is indeed to parse and contrast among things to reconstruct what they might mean. We segregate what
is or is not of the "same." In his seminal book *Principles of Psychology* (1890),
William James already noted that the sense of sameness "is the very keel and
backbone of our thinking"[1] (p. 459). We should add to this that the sense of
sameness is necessarily always co-determined with the sense of what is *different*, the other side of the coin.

What we are constantly doing in our head is tracking what is of the same
and, hence, also what is different. I will propose that actually the latter, although co-determined, is having precedence over the former in the basic
process of categorization. Objects, for example, can only be perceived if we
are able to contrast and segregate them as *different* from a ground. Likewise,
in the social and moral domain what we mainly do in our heads is to segregate by contrast and to identify what is of the same by primarily opposing
and focusing on what is different, clumping exemplars into categories: foes as
opposed to friends, bad guys versus good guys, analogous to the differentia-
tion of figure and ground that is core to object perception. This simple prop-
osition entails that, psychologically, we are biased toward highlighting things
primarily via a process of segregation, a necessary process ingrained in our
biology and the way our brain works.

---

[1] James, W. (1890/1950). *The principles of psychology*. New York, NY: Dover.

Moral Acrobatics. Philippe Rochat, Oxford University Press (2021). © Oxford University Press.
DOI: 10.1093/oso/9780190057657.003.0010

We are born with what we might call an "exclusivity instinct," in the broad sense of sorting things by exclusion of what is *not* of the same, which also necessarily results in the detection of what is of the same category, as noted by William James. Both are inseparable and co-determined processes, yet psychologically and particularly in the social and moral realm, the former (exclusion) tends to have precedence over the latter (inclusion).

Exclusive by nature, we tend to parse primarily by attrition and subtraction (i.e., by exclusion rather than inclusion). In the social and moral domain, the determination of what is of the same tends to be mainly the result of an eliminative rather than an inclusive process of categorization. Plainly put, in the social domain eliminative processes seem to dominate. As for body guards, it is somehow easier for us to block people at the red VIP cord than giving them a pass. Exclusivity obliges.

Striking is the fact that our perceptions and conceptualization of what we construe as "fair," for example, is typically defined on an eliminative basis of what is "unfair." Fairness is referred first to what is *not*. Children starting to grapple with the notion of fairness do point first and foremost at what is "unfair!" Children will not start grappling with the notion by claiming equity, pointing to what is equitable, or spontaneously claiming "That's fair!" Rather (think of the too common sibling rivalries over possession, treats, or food sharing), they will primarily protest to what they see as "unfair!" Parents might elaborate with their notion of fairness, not kids. Fairness, like any other elusive concept, tends to be categorized primarily by contrast and elimination of what it is not. This asymmetry prevails, particularly in the social and moral domain.

The feeling of entitlement over things and people (i.e., exclusivity to self) is a building-block propensity in our ways of dealing with others, particularly evident in the context of family feuds, often the most ferocious.[2] Case in point is the endless Israeli–Palestinian conflict, a conflict between people that share the same historical roots, whose religious practices and beliefs are in many ways very close. Family feuds tend to be the worse and the most lethal. They demonstrate the heightened, primary sense of entitlement developed among close kin and other chosen alliances (husband and wife, lovers). The force of such entitlement can be measured in the too common cases of irreconcilable resentments between divorcees, typically crystallizing over

---

[2] See Rochat, P. (2014). *Origins of possession: Owning and sharing in development.* Cambridge, England: Cambridge University Press.

money, or the heightened feuds over material asset inheritance spent paying attorney fees, an absurd outcome. Economically nonsensical, it does serve some deep symbolic and subjective purpose for the kin foes. Rumors say that one third of all last wills and family successions in France end up contested and ruled by a tribunal!

Competition over things, rivalry, and the fear of losing undivided attention from parents and primary caretakers form a default, basic value system we all share. It is part of the human biological make-up, the foundation of kinship alliance as basic societal unit. This is true across cultures, where the kinship family unit is more or less distributed within the collectivity (e.g., nuclear unit vs. more communal parenting like in kibbutz or small-scale traditional societies). All of us are born with the deep need for exclusive control and a sense of entitlement to undivided attention from caretakers.

The devastating effects of chronic child neglect found in crowded and impoverished orphanages during and following political turmoil such as what happened in Romania in the early 1990s testifies to the fact that without the possibility of literally "feeding" the need for exclusivity, children are arrested in their development. Without exclusivity, the possibility of being a privileged object of attention and having agency over others' attention—in other words, without receiving adequate care aside from being physically fed—no children survive unscathed from their prolonged immaturity and protracted dependence on others that are two basic characteristics of human ontogeny.

In development, the primary context in which exclusivity is expressed is sibling and other kin rivalry. Freud and his use of the Oedipus myth (rivalry between father and son over the mother) as a basic tension in the shaping the human person is not far off the mark. The Oedipus drama and tension echoes something that is biologically real, although needs to be enlarged to all kinship, not just the parents.

Early in life, on the part of the infant, there is always the irresistible quest for reassuring undivided attention and recognition from mother and other primary caretakers. It is a primary motivational core in spherical norm creation and binding. It is a binding that—from the start—functions based on an exclusion rather than an inclusion principle. It is primarily *to the exclusion of others*. It is nurtured eventually to become more inclusive, but from the outset, it is exclusive.

This exclusion principle is the source mechanism of moral compartmentalization and spherical alliance formation. It is fundamentally driven by a universal struggle for recognition from others, an essential self-reassuring drive. Universally, we all live and depend on the evaluative gaze of others, constantly gauging our own value and place in the social world, craving recognition and positive evaluation from others. Without such gaze—in particular, positive gaze from others—we become worthless and helpless; we lose both power and agency. This is specific to humans, the only species that engages in the cultivation of impression management, wearing makeup and other accessories, doing almost anything for just 15 minutes of fame.

Spontaneous social binding and alliance creation rest on mutual recognition. As we know, paying attention to others pays in our social conquest. It is part of any good seduction tips, the main avenue to receiving sympathy and recognition from others in a process of mutual social recognition. The exclusive and untamed gaze of the other upon the self in mutual recognition is what precipitates love chemistry, the source of exclusive passions. Being ignored by someone can also be the source of commensurate obsession and devastation, especially if a nonmutual crush befalls on us.

Aside from kinship and spontaneous social binding arising from love infatuation, extreme circumstances may create paradoxical alliances. There are circumstantial co-dependencies like the alliance between torturer and victim, master and slave, or in co-abusive relationships like the one famously portrayed in Edward Albee play *Who's Afraid of Virginia Woolf?* These paradoxical alliances rest on a radically different sort of mutual recognition. It is a recognition that is forced upon the protagonists by perverted circumstances, a corrupted or distorted expression of spontaneous social binding, from which they can't extricate themselves. Forced alliances are by definition a perversion, the alteration of something from its original course or meaning.

Love and jealousy form exclusive values attached to spontaneous alliances only, not forced alliances. The love of victims toward their torturers, of slave to their master, is a myth. Such sadistic love is misconstrued for the fact that torturer and victim, master and slave, are linked in a relation that co-defines their respective roles, a relation in which they co-exist and their respective role is co-dependent (as discussed by the young Hegel). But the lusting of victims for their torturer, and vice versa, is probably just a perverted fantasy. I don't think any torturer really lusts to cause pain or that any victims secretly enjoy being tortured. Sadomasochistic sex practices are reinforcing for their transgression and exploration of roles, as well as of trust, a genuinely enticing and harmless play for some. But, in reality, such play has nothing to do with the actual perversion of real torture. They correspond more to spontaneous alliances as in a temporary exclusive relationship. Nobody forces anybody to visit a sex dungeon. Both real victims and their real torturers do not choose to visit the torture chamber, irrespective of their role. It is doubtful that real torturers actually enjoy torturing. In the 2003 infamous Abu Ghraib prison pictures, as seen in the reproduced picture below (Figure 10.1), or other atrocious photographs of lynching in the South of the United States or elsewhere in the world, witness participants and active torturers might grin and joke during the act, but those are more expressions of defense and coping mechanisms. It is doubtful that it has anything to do with the plain expression of lust and pleasure one has in a pay-for-sex dungeon.

For child and comparative psychologists, imprinting is considered a main source mechanism of affective parsing and the formation of social predilection. This mechanism corresponds, at the most basic level, to rapid learning and bonding creation by mere exposure during a sensitive period. Across species, imprinting is the primitive social glue, a central piece of newborns' survival kit. As first documented by ethologist Konrad Lorentz

Figure 10.1 Smeared prisoner at Abu Ghraib Prison.
© Randy McMahon 2013.

(b. 1903–d. 1989), hatching chicks of avian species happen to latch on the first moving objects they see, be it human, a mechanical toy, or the biological mother. Basic cares in terms of food, warmth, and protection depend on rapid imprinting, younglings able to track and latch on these indispensable resources without which they would not survive outside the egg or maternal womb.

This automatic imprinting process tends to occur first during the earliest stage of posthatching or postnatal development, creating what would correspond to an individual's basic affective nucleus. It shapes the primordial affective investment toward a primary caretaker. This investment turns into a lasting attachment pattern that varies depending on the species: immediate and predictable in most species, longer to establish and more variable in humans.

Early imprinting and affective bonding can have enduring effects, determining, for example, adult sexual preference as in the case of captive animals selectively courting the human captors who raised them. Touching images of Panda bears clinging to their human caretakers are viral on the Internet, and, as already mentioned, rat pups exposed to their mother with a particular perfume will later prefer mating with females wearing the same scent. In humans, there is good empirical evidence also demonstrating that the early imprinting or attachment pattern serves as representational template or "working model" for later selected social bonds, the selection of sexual partners and friends beyond the close biological circle of primary caretakers.

Many obstacles to early imprinting exist, however, especially if there are multiple siblings born at the same time, as in the case of twins, or when older siblings are still breastfed by the mother. Rivalry and competition for care is a universal conundrum in humans but also in nature in general, from sparrows, to rats, to monkeys. Affective resources are limited, often scarce for the young. This is true especially for us humans, a source of heightened rivalry tensions and in-group competition because of our prolonged developmental immaturity and protracted dependence on maternal care. The human dependence on others to survive is unmatched in nature and probably what makes us from the outset among the most jealous, defensive, and truly revengeful creature there is. It is also part of a proclivity leading us, as members of a self-conscious species, to cooperate, to care about reputation, and to end up having normative morals.

A link exists between an original exclusivity instinct driving social behavior and thinking the world in black and white (categorical thinking and moral compartmentalization). Again, to display affective predilections and seek exclusive alliances with others is to parse the social world in terms of a binary value system, fundamentally following an approach-avoidance polarity principle. "Magnetic" attraction/repulsion forces, or +/- polarity, is a universal value opposition in both the living and physical world. In both worlds, any force entails some resistance or reaction. Inanimate physical objects as well as animate sentient entities like us exist by virtue of a temporary state of equilibrium between opposite forces that hold atoms or "stuff" together, as well as their temporary situation in space like a vase on a table or a shelf holding it in place (-) against the force of gravity (+). The same polarity and always temporary kind of equilibrium exist between approach-avoidance forces driving all animals from amoebas to primates. This basic principle applies to human affective life from the outset.

Infants from the start, and even as fetuses in the womb, are more or less attracted to perceptual features they quickly latch on and, inversely, nonattractive features they avoid or reject. From the outset, we build physical and social expectations, calibrating the range of our subjective experience. We build our own tolerance and level of avoidant responses to aversive, unexpected stimulations like loud sounds, salty smell, or bright light. Each individual newborn regulates his or her emotions differently, displaying various degrees of reactivity and calming following a stressful event, evidence of variable starting state temperaments. Research show that from at least six weeks postpartum, infants become attuned and selective of the ways familiar people interact with them, the way they talk, look, smile, and the timing of their engagement in face-to-face exchanges.

Infants become rapidly more attentive and responsive to familiar primary caretakers with whom they typically manage to develop exclusive alliances (mother, father, sibling). Within weeks, infants become weary of strangers and are comforted by familiar individuals.[3] They parse their social world based on specific value systems expressed in terms of attraction and weariness. Once again, we are born in a world of values, driven by the need to reinforce exclusive alliances with some individuals over others. There is an

---

[3] Rochat, P. (2004). *The infant's world* (Rev. ed.). Cambridge, MA: Harvard University Press.

instinctual proclivity expressed in the human young to seek attention and se-lectively promote affective attunement. From the outset, the premium value is controlling others' attention and affective investment toward the self,[4] in a context of competition (exclusivity seeking) and always by exclusion.

As we will see next, because exclusivity and exclusion are typically tied to love and infatuation, they are also always detrimental to those they neces-sarily exclude.

[4] Rochat, P. (2013). The gaze of others. In M. Banaji & S. Gelman (Eds), *Navigating the social world*. New York, NY: Oxford University Press.

11

Love as Exclusion

The starting point of any psychology is to ask how we create values for ourselves. What makes us prefer this person over that person? This thing over that thing? What is the source of our likes and dislikes? A fundamental psychological question is indeed how one gets bounded and affectively attached to certain people and things, over other people and other things. Because it has the incommensurable potential to foster war, ethnic cleansing, bullying, ostracism, and other social devastations of rejection and the systematic elimination of others, it raises a simple psychological question: Why does our infatuations with others always tend to be associated with the systematic rejection of others and, hence, always to the detriment of others? Why are exclusion and compartmentalization the necessary corollaries of social bonding? In other words, why is love typically exclusive? To answer this question, it is necessary to look into the origins of affective investments, starting with some basic processes manifested from the outset of development.

Inscribed into our psychic system are affective imprinting processes. These processes are the original source of differential investment and quick binding toward certain things over others. It always takes place in favor of a selected few. It is the process by which from birth we select and differentially invest our affects into particular persons or groups, as well as so-called transitional objects such as dolls and blankets that babies often get attached to from the first year. It is the basic process by which we start parsing our social world along affinities, distinguishing comfort and prediction linked to the familiar as opposed to the unfamiliar. Inversely, and by extension, it is also the source of our dislikes and potential for dehumanizing of unfamiliar people. We draw strict, categorical lines in our valuation of people, from sacred to trash. If we love our children and immediate family, it is by exclusion. The fact is that love, by definition, is selective. It is always to the detriment of others outside of the particular sphere of infatuation. This is too often overlooked. The simple rule is that things in our mind can only exist via a process of exclusion and the enhancement of contrast in relation to all others. Exclusion is the seed of why we think the world in black and white. Alliance exists because

Moral Acrobatics. Philippe Rochat, Oxford University Press (2021). © Oxford University Press.
DOI: 10.1093/oso/9780190057657.003.0011

of rejection, in the same way that love exists inversely because of hate—no contrast, no existence, as simple as that. Instinctively, we create contrasts to navigate the social world.

From birth, we compartmentalize affective investments in relation to what we perceive and associate with particular feeling experiences. We prefer interacting with certain people over others; we are attracted to certain things and people over other things and people. Again, as a necessary counterpart of such an inclusive positive "preference" process, there is exclusion, still begging the fundamental question of what might drive such a process.

Objects of predilection are typically associated with greater comfort and safety. Inversely, threat and insecurity are associated with objects of repulsion. Stated differently, objects of predilection yield necessarily to the contrasting characterization of those that should be avoided, associated with potentially greater stress and threat. By necessity, affective predilection and infatuation entails rejection and selective disliking. Falling in love entails exclusivity and, hence, is always to the detriment of discarded others. It eliminates other potential objects of love and infatuation.

At a group level, rejection is clearly a central process as it tends to reinforce in-group bonding. This is evident in the recurrent cases of political fanaticism that feed the news. A good and more mundane example is when a red cordon separates the chosen VIP group from the ordinaries (as in most discos, theaters, or airline lounges). A general exclusivity rule applies based on wealth, looks, and reputation. When the cordon is too loose and, hence, too inclusive, the value of its function drops. It loses its charm as snobs would say. Too much inclusiveness does indeed reduce the exclusivity value of those admitted behind the red cord.

From the cradle of development, within weeks, infants build an affective capital made of exclusive attachment with some individuals to the exclusion of others. This simple, primordial fact is at the root of what will eventually become the compartmentalizing of moral spheres within which different standards and norms apply. From birth, all we do is primarily create values in interaction with others, not only in positive but also negative ways. We hunt for positive feedbacks, struggling for signs of recognition from others, often probing such recognition by creating tensions, dramas, gossips, or bullying.

The propensity to create dramas and tensions with others serves the same basic and very human function of gauging our own place and value in relation to others. We gauge the evaluative gaze toward the self through drama creation and tension with selected others, not unlike two-year-olds running faster toward the busy street or the deep end of the swimming pool as their mother screams louder in panic. Our main trade is indeed to create evaluative contexts and social situations that are value boosting for the self, constantly reassuring and consolidating our self-identity, including the group we happen to identify with, whether family, nationality, faith, ethnicity, or the team we are rooting for.

This self-evaluative meta-conceptual lens helps us to make some sense of what might be the developmental origins of human moral compartmentalization, our double moral standards, and allied hypocrisies, in other words what might be the roots of how we tend to think the world in black and white to avoid ethical ambiguities.

As already mentioned, reputation comes from the Latin verb *putare* or "to calculate." It stands for the calculation of others' evaluation of us as individuals (me, you) or groups (my family, my team, my party, my "race"). This calculation is a preoccupation that is unique to our species. Sociopaths apart, our reputation always tends to follow us. It is constantly hovering in our mind. From at least two to three years of age, we mainly exist through the evaluative eyes of others. The human exacerbated care for reputation is also inseparable from a unique propensity to compartmentalize the social world in terms of separate value systems and double standards, as exemplified by Hitler's vegetarianism or Ariel Castro's love for his daughter. It is also inseparable from our exacerbated propensity toward duplicity, lies, and self-deception. The logic behind such assertion and the general intuition is that we humans, unlike any other animals, are self-conscious. We feed off of others' approbation like no other species does. Simply defined, self-consciousness corresponds here to the construal by individuals of themselves and their place in the world as an object of evaluation through both their own eyes, but also invariably through the evaluative eyes of others. Self-consciousness would bring about the human unmatched capacity for duplicity and moral compartmentalization.

It is in self-consciousness that we find the root of multiple affective value systems that co-exist in our minds, enacted depending on context: the context of specific social alliances such as family, nationality, team, church, political organization, army, or any professional institution. In the context of each sphere, we embody various roles, abiding to particular expectations, dancing to particular, often radically different tunes. We switch from one to the other, one standard to another, from moment to moment, place to place, situation to situation.

For each role we seek different kinds of recognition linked to specific expectations and particular metrics for being good in that particular role: good father in the presence of children, good child in the presence of mother, good lover in the presence of those we fall for, good worker in the presence of the boss, good soldier on the front. Each corresponds to different standards, different role-playing rules dictated by the particular spherical alliance (family, lover, employer, army). Each spherical role embodies particular morals or value systems: Hitler the dictator, the painter, the son, the animal, the lover.

The remarkable fact of human self-conscious life is indeed our unmatched ability to switch roles effortlessly, unphased by what often amounts to blatant, irreconcilable moral etiquettes. We manage to compartmentalize these roles, hermetically enough to prevent self-implosion. Pressure toward compartmentalization appears to be linked to our ingrained monitoring of others, our insatiable need for approbation as we navigate through spheres that often tend to be mutually exclusive. As a rule, alliances always exist to the exclusion of others, to the detriment of some others. De facto, alliances and ostracism are two sides of the same coin: a necessarily, yet too often denied, Janus-faced coin.

Aside from the dark side of any alliances (i.e., exclusion), another deep conundrum associated with human self-consciousness is to figure out what is the head wearing all those moral hats? Who is Hitler? The pet lover, vegetarian, or the mass killer? Who is Castro? The loving son, father, or sexual deviant and abductor. At a less dramatic scale, the various moral contexts of each of our typically more mundane alliances also carry different expectations and metrics through which we navigate and in our social lives, always trying to maintain some sort of coherent moral identity. If not for a third-party observer, it is at least true that we manage to hold some moral coherence in our own head to the extent that we typically avoid paralysis and implosion under the weight of often blatant contradictions and ensuing guilt. With our juggling of roles and their various metrics, we manage making our contradictions bearable, avoiding sphere implosion as in the case of fictive John. We manage to compartmentalize our roles as parent, lover, pet owner, parishioner, friend, fighter, drill sergeant, boss, employee, boot camper, or care provider.

Our alliances tend to carry their own ruling and etiquette norms. They often entail radically different value systems (family man vs. fierce soldier or harsh competitor). These systems rest on compartmentalized morals and standards, often difficult to reconcile, often under pressure of possible implosion, as in the fictive case of John.

Lies and self-deception are mechanisms by which we avoid sphere collapses under the weight of inherent moral ambiguities. We avoid facing the reality that any alliance is always based on both centripetal (inclusion) and centrifugal force (exclusion). This complementary process entails inherent moral ambiguities and contradictions: the centripetal force of exclusive love that brings us together, and the centrifugal force that makes us kill to protect our progenies and ostracize in fear of losing in-group unity.

Hitler's uncanny combination, on one hand, of militant vegetarianism, vocal nature lover, and animal protector, and, on the other, of being the unmatched mass murderer and the prototype of mad and bad is not easy to fathom. It appears however to be analogous, albeit at a vastly different scale, to the expression of a process of moral compartmentalization and the balance of dual centripetal and centrifugal forces that we all share, within and between our various social spheres. In general, such a process is what appears to hold all of our moral character and identity together, preventing us from collapsing under the weight of our own contradictions.

12

Belonging Instinct

Behind our moral acrobatics, the topic of this book, there is first and foremost a deeply ingrained need to belong with select others, to create trust in a close bond and to act accordingly. Moral ambiguities are indirect spin-off and symbolic expressions of the instinct to fulfill this need, the basic expression of our ingrained sociality, the fact that from the outset without others we are nothing. We cannot survive.

People do need people; in particular, they need to belong and be recognized as integral member of a group or community. Nothing is worse than being transparent to the gaze of others. We affirm and constantly probe our place via the co-existing and co-defining proclivities of inclusion and exclusion of the self in relation to others (dual centripetal and centrifugal forces). Constantly seeking reassurance of our own exclusivity in the eyes of a selected few (reputation), we systematically promote and sustain our own relative inclusiveness by exclusion and subtraction of selected others who are filtered out in the process. This process is universal. It applies equally for those protecting their inclusion privilege, such as belonging to a select group or trying to acquire membership privilege. Think of Third World immigrants with their accent and surface physic in a First World country trying to find their place as new citizens (centripetal force), while under the skeptic and fearful "entitled" look of all the earlier legal immigrants protecting their own privilege, their hard-earned comfort zone (centrifugal force). Both forces are complementary, under the same fundamental umbrella drive: the need to belong. This need drives relations of self to others from birth, and it is not just motivated by breast or access to food.

We are born well equipped to develop affective co-dependence and ultimately what constitutes our primary sense of belonging that, by the second year of life, our symbolic and self-reflective mind takes off for recursive spinoffs. First, we bond with our mother and then expand this bond to larger groups. There is a built-in, powerful, and organizing need from the outset to affiliate with others, a basic drive to capture care and attention from others, managing intimacy first with mother, rapidly expanding this original

Moral Acrobatics. Philippe Rochat, Oxford University Press (2021). © Oxford University Press.
DOI: 10.1093/oso/9780190057657.003.0012

affective alliance to selected others. Deep in us and from the outset, we express a belonging instinct: the irresistible propensity to partake and share experiences with others. This instinct is primary to psychic life.

As with birds, rats, or monkeys, the need for attachment is rooted in biology, much more than simply a need to be fed. Newborns need physical proximity, intimacy, and warmth. Aside from food, they equally feed on affection from others. Capturing the attention of others and bonding with them are essential parts of our survival kit.

The seminal observations in orphanages of abandoned children by child psychiatrist René Spitz collected immediately after the World War II demonstrated the devastating effects of affective neglect on young infants homed in overcrowded institutions. Receiving food but deprived of exclusive care and attention, Spitz filmed these kids and documented a syndrome (hospitalism) by which these infants and young children literally shut down in their development. They withdraw within themselves, rocking repetitively and engaging in circular self-soothing behaviors that are characteristic of low-functioning autistic children. The main symptom of autism is social disconnection and a blindness toward the mind of others. The same observations have been replicated in recent years across multiple orphanages of war-torn countries from all over the world.

The famous—for many, infamous—laboratory observations of Harry Harlow in the 1960s with rhesus macaques also demonstrate dramatically the social dependency need of the newborn infant, aside from the indispensable dispensing of food from the maternal breast. Harlow and collaborators captured in vivo the predictable deleterious effect of social isolation from the caregiving practices and companionship of the mother. Separate from their mother at birth, Harlow raised the young monkeys in captivity with two artificial mesh-made mothers wearing fake googled eyes. One fed the infant via a bottle attached to it, as the other was just covered with a piece of soft cloth. Harlow made his point by showing that infants clung seeking comfort and spent significantly more time with the soft surrogate mother compared to the feeding mother, especially when facing threats like a loud noise or someone approaching their cage. Early affective bonding was evident above and beyond the physical need of being fed or to suck, above and beyond what Freud suggested in his early psychoanalytical writings on primitive pulsions and infantile sexuality. Spitz's observations[1] and Harlow's

---

[1] Spitz, R. A. (1965). *The first year of life: A psychoanalytic study of normal and deviant development of object relations.* New York, NY: Basic Books.

works[2] triggered massive research on attachment from the 1960s on, spearheaded primarily by John Bowlby and Mary Ainsworth[3] who demonstrated the universal importance of early human bonding to the primary caretaker. They also triggered a large body of research suggesting a relatively small number of attachment forms (e.g., secure, insecure, or disorganized) between children and their primary caretaker, these forms tending to be reproduced through adulthood with chosen partners. These attachment forms appear to be like imprinted relational working models for the individual. It eventually shapes each individual's predilection for certain forms of attachment or alliances with others later in life. For attachment theorists, these various forms of alliance explain, for example, marked differences in how individuals cope and express anxiety over separation, in other words the fear of losing control over others as objects of attachment.

Separation anxiety is indeed a major psychological conundrum from birth on. It shapes our trust in people. It is an ingrained fear that carries increasing weight as the child becomes self-conscious and grapples with the inevitability of death: the ultimate vanishing of self, the horrifying feasibility of an absolute separation from others forever. It is the projection of terminal abandonment from others, what Stanley Kubrick's *2001: A Space Odyssey* conveys in the scene of an astronaut, walking in space, and suddenly sucked into the infinity of the cosmos, the cord to the mother station ruptured.

We are born prepared to bond and receive care from others, except that by the second year of life, things change when the child becomes symbolic and self-conscious. With the workings of the imagination, the emergence of language and other pretense abilities, such need rapidly becomes symbolic and self-conscious. It opens the door to the phantasm of bonding with others and groups above and beyond the original working model of attachment to primary caretaker(s).

The first feeding experience and the particularities of first encounters with the multisensory care from the mother or any primary caretaker must be thought of as a primary imprinting source. This primary imprinting source becomes referential to our own affective calibration in relation to others, the roots of our social comfort zone and varied way we eventually come into contact with others and create bonds with them. The road from the dynamic of first social alliance with primary caretaker to the diversity of adults'

---

[2] Harlow, H. F. (1958). The nature of love. *American Psychologist, 13,* 673–685.
[3] Ainsworth, M., & Bowlby, J. (1965). *Child care and the growth of love.* London, England: Penguin Books.

ways in creating affiliation with others—in other words, their characters or personalities—is certainly not a simple causal trajectory. The chemistry of innate temperaments and proclivities that each of the protagonists brings to the alliance is impossible to predict really, including chaotic bifurcations as a function of multiple extraneous and unpredictable factors, or chance encounters. To start with, we all depend on the place and time of our birth, our developmental niche: the inherited chance circumstances of our coming to life at that particular place, at that particular time, from that particular gene pool of people struggling to survive within their own inherited circumstances.

The whole process is intrinsically stochastic. Yet there are unmistakable stable patterns. Whatever the niche, all individuals get attached and bind with others, first mainly to individual others, quickly enlarging such attachment to groups. Even by becoming irresistibly gregarious and crowd suckers, we never lose our inclination for individual attachments, naturally and effortlessly creating a cleavage between the two kinds of alliance sphere, as elusive as the boundaries of these kinds might be: the private sphere and the public or collective sphere. This distinction is transcultural, expressed in all societies, varying only in the way it is expressed, often aggregated in particular social practices and cultural tools marking public versus private spheres, like the *tu* versus *vous* forms in French, the *du* versus *sie* in German.

All through life, we remain in need of interpersonal intimacy, feeding our private interpersonal sphere. With friends, lovers, and offspring, we tend to recreate the quality of our original bond to the mother. We are "communing" with select others. In the meantime, we are also quickly pulled to enlarge this bond rapidly adding more public and encompassing spheres. Within months, and certainly by preschool age (three to five years old), children start creating and participating to greater alliances, outside of their immediate family. They bond with other individuals in less intimate contexts.

The juggling of private and public spheres is a constant in our lives. Each represents various forms of alliance, various degrees of trust, expectations, and commitment. Each sphere carries with it different *standards* that need to switch as we navigate back and forth from one sphere to another: family, lovers, friends, co-workers, team members, political affiliates, war enemies, party members, members of other social segments, races, ethnicities. These spheres often rest on deeply contradictory value systems, as in the extreme cases of Castro or Hitler. Serial killers might spend intimate and genuinely loving time with their mother or child and then seamlessly switching to horrendous victimizing modes.

All children develop to be sustainable moral acrobats, able to switch moral codes and cover up contradictions while keeping face, as in the production of "polite" white lies from around three years of age. What drives it all is the basic need to affiliate, a bonding instinct expressed from birth and the same driving force that is symbolically expressed in complex, often ambiguous ways in our adult lives as we struggle to build a reputation, have an impact, struggle to be loved and recognized by others. This struggle is universal, mass murderers and other deviant souls included.

The depth and universality of human belonging instinct is probably best revealed by our ways of punishing, since the beginning of human recorded history in all societies. All punishments have in common, one way or another, the practice of starving the binding instinct via social exclusion, imprisonment, and solitary confinement, with sometime the ultimate threat of death, the absolute severance of the individual from the group.

In Western societies, and now all over the world, caning and other public physical tortures have been replaced with prison time, the psychological punishment by isolation from the larger group, the condemnation to do penitence in institutional confinement (i.e., penitentiary) with other penitents. If penitents become recidivists during incarceration, a criminal among other criminals, they are universally condemned to solitary confinement where they spend time alone, socially deprived. If they persist in their transgression while in solitary confinement, individuals are punished by being physically eliminated: the absolute isolation from the group, the "capital" punishment still practiced in many countries.

The universal tool of isolation of the individual from the group is an inverse demonstration of the centrality of our belonging instinct. Isolation from the main group, in any society around the world, is found to be the major tool of payback imposed on the individual. It is the revenge tool of choice in any society and the main instrument of deterrence to preserve social harmony, across highly different human cultures. In the still highly traditional small-scale society of Samoa in the South Pacific, the worse and most dreaded punishment for crimes as grave as murders is not to be locked up in a Western-style facility, but to be expelled from the native village, ultimately creating shame to the extended family. In Samoa, those expelled always end up adopted by a neighbor village, sometime less than a mile away. The fear of rejection is indeed universal, a powerful and commensurate inverse of our insatiable instinct to belong. It is also a major piece of what's behind our moral ambiguities.

PART 3

MECHANISMS

What Shapes Our Moral Decisions?

The fear of rejection and allied psychological insecurities is revealing of our primarily self-protective moralizing and own moral blind spots as we shall see in the next series of chapters (Part 3, Mechanisms). These chapters focus on some of the major psychological mechanisms that shape our moral decisions, misleading us toward inequity, strong biases, self-deception, stereotyping, and other convenient shortcuts.

13

Blind Spots and Shortcuts

The blind spots in our eyes are the holes on the retina where the optic nerve exits to connect with the brain. It is blind because at this location there are no receptor cells, therefore no possible visual stimulation. Yet, the brain fills the gap by inferring what the eye would see at this spot, were there cell photoreceptors at that location. This inference is made from adjacent cell stimulations. As a result, we do not perceive our blind spots as a black hole, as we should objectively. There is no interruption in what we perceive. It is continuous. This is a ghostly perception, a trick evolved by our brain to support more efficient adaptation to a complex and continuous visual environment made of dangers and sparse resources.

Such brain extrapolations are endemic; the reality we perceive is never literal but a transformation from the get-go, essentially a reliable, for the most part invariant and adaptive inference by our nervous system of what is out there. The most striking demonstration of such adaptive inference not only in the realm of vision, but also in other sense modalities, are classic optical illusions. For example, we see the moon much bigger when close to the horizon than when at the zenith, high in the sky perpendicular to where you are on the earth's surface. It demonstrates that our perception is rarely absolute. It is for the most part context dependent and circumstantial, made of automatic and unconscious inferences, what corresponds in essence to implicit extrapolations. These immediate extrapolations are shortcuts or perceptual heuristics that connect the dots, creating ghostly meanings such as continuity when there is none, continuous apparent motion when two lamps flash in regular alternation. There are objectively two lamps in the environment, but we infer one lamp jumping back and forth. Realizing how much reconstruction there is in how we view the world is both humbling and quite unsettling. Indeed, one may ask, what is real?

Discovering that the two horizontal segments of the Müller–Lyer illusion that the moon at different elevations are actually of absolute same dimension or seeing the concave side of a facial mask becoming suddenly convex as it

Moral Acrobatics. Philippe Rochat, Oxford University Press (2021). © Oxford University Press.
DOI: 10.1093/oso/9780190057657.003.0013

rotates (the famous mask illusion[1]), all of these phenomena point to the ines-capable fact that a lot of what we see are brain tricks, the result of error-prone heuristics that we can't avoid, no matter how aware we might be of such tricks. "Our mind is f**** with us!" as one stunned student bluntly screamed out at one of my large perception class.

The misleading effects of illusions are to a large extent obligatory and es-sentially hard to shake. This is why some radical philosophers of mind, like Jerry Fodor, suggest that the mind's work is built around primary ready-made modules that force us to see and parse the world in a certain way. This idea has a long tradition, starting with German 18th-century enlightenment philosopher Immanuel Kant (b. 1724–d. 1804) who wrote about inescapable formats or categories of our thinking, suggesting that much of our thoughts are relative to those obligatory ways our mind evolved to parse the world. Much of our awareness about the world is indeed the product of obligatory illusions, particularly in the moral domain, a minefield of implicit biases, obligatory blind spots, "connecting the dots" heuristics leading us astray from more balanced and compassionate decisions, attitudes, and judgments not only about others but also about ourselves.

To draw a further analogy with basic perceptual mechanisms, another unsettling phenomenon naturally happens at the level of our retina. I men-tion it because it demonstrates that obligatory illusions are pervasive, even at the most primary level of our sensory processing, from the moment physical energy from the outside world, such as light, hits the surface of our receptors. At that moment, this energy (light, sound pressure, airborne molecules) gets transduced or transformed into a nerve impulse (literally a digitizing process into on/off signals) for further brain treatment that feeds our awareness of the real (i.e., what we perceive and our making sense of the world). In this primary process, in the realm of vision in particular, there is a so-called lat-eral inhibition phenomenon. In vision, when a light source hits one of the photoreceptor cells that pave the retina, connections automatically *inhibit* the receptivity of neighbor cells, hence the term *lateral inhibition*. This pro-cess results in virtually enhancing contrasts for further processing by higher structures of the visual cortex. Such primary filtering and contrast, which is de facto a categorical amplification process that recreates or represents what

---

[1] For such top–down accounts of perceptual illusions, see the compelling works and hypothet-ical theories in Rock, I. (1983). *The logic of perception*. Cambridge, MA: MIT Press, as well as the classic Gregory, R. L. (1966). *Eye and brain: The psychology of seeing*. Princeton, NJ: Princeton University Press.

is out there in the world, has an analog in all other perceptual modalities. It is a fundamental invariant of how our perceptions work.

Lateral inhibition is another striking example that already at the level of our retina, visual information is naturally filtered whereby the raw light energy signal that is captured and transduced into nerve impulse by photoreceptor cells is somehow Photoshopped for further processing. From the most primary level of processing, what we see of the world are enhanced brain representations, like those high-contrast chromo pictures amateur photographers overmanicure with available software to generate compelling effects.

The question remains, of course, as to what is an accurate representation of reality—What contrasts capture it best? There is obviously no absolute answer to that question, and this is exactly the issue we are dealing with here in relation to morality. How can we approximate wiser moral decisions by being more "realistic" and less biased in our categorical filtering of the social world?

The first step is for us to own the fact not only of our implicit, but also our explicit biased ways of categorically representing the world. We should first and foremost acknowledge the fact that no one is immune to blind-spot phenomena and obligatory illusions, from primary perception to higher level moral decisions. To tame such biases and eventually become morally wiser, more just, and more balanced in our judgments of self and others, it is necessary first to own them, an unsettling and humbling process that this book is trying to promote.

Everything in nature has been selected over time following the Darwinian precepts of natural selection. Such selection accounts for the existence of current forms (structural organization) and functions (behaviors) that are observable in all living things. Moral blind spots and shortcuts do not escape such evolutionary reality. If they exist, we have to conclude that it was for some survival gain, selected for their adaptive benefit. In the case of blind spots and categorical shortcuts, one of the selective benefits was to smooth and facilitate our navigation of the social world, yet enabling much moral dilemma. But nature dictated that to survive we can't afford being constantly torn in moral procrastination. We have to move on in our moral and ethical decisions, most of the time not even thinking too much about it. If, for example, each time I decided to tip someone I had to rationally factor the personal situation of that person, I would not get much traction in my life. The shortcut is 20% tip unless the service was bad. We live off such heuristics that facilitate our lives but end up blinding ourselves as moral agents. It increases our distance to people. There is something to be said about making efforts in getting closer to people as we make moral decisions. This is an endless process but a process that can be marked with progress, trying to overcome our default ways of looking at and assessing people.

Treating people as people, making an effort to see them as persons and not just disposable objects, goes a long way. Clearly, there is a marked difference between encountering a bum on the street (possibly handing him a coin or a cigarette) and taking the time to inquire how this person feels or, at minimum, acknowledging this person's existence with eye contact, a head nod, or a simple "Hi!" But in our busy lives, we can't procrastinate and have to move on making swift decisions. Shortcuts, categorical biases, and other blind spots facilitate our social navigation. However, this adaptation is often at much ethical cost. Seeing persons rather than objects in people is a moral prerequisite, and there are no limits to the progress each of us can do in this realm. The same applies to non-human animals.

Perpetrators of extreme collective violence, those who kill hundreds or are trained torturers, engage in a systematic dehumanizing process. They are trained to shut off any person or personal perception of their victims. They kill them like throwing out trash, treating them as objects. In a collective rage context, dehumanizing is an adaptive process. Dehumanizing or humanizing processes are learnable and plastic, and no one can pretend to escape them. Deprograming the dehumanizing process taking place at the time of conflicts is possible, yet can be very traumatic for perpetrators trying to own what they were capable of doing during the collective rage epidemic. Humanizing and dehumanizing processes can be reversed in both ways. With practice, doctors learn to de-empathize, hence dehumanize, their suffering patients when it comes down to performing surgery and treating them as physical bodies. They manage to suspend their personal, empathic perception to focus exclusively on the body repair. But the reverse is also possible, becoming more attuned to people as people, like humanizing street bums as we walk by them.

Recent studies point to our flipping humanizing/dehumanizing ways of perceiving strangers as either good or bad persons. This perception depends on very rudimentary pieces of information. Our ways of perceiving others, in particular their faces, are implicitly framed by previous cues with deeply ingrained semantic associations. These associations shape our social attitudes and immediate judgments, our immediate "feeling" or first impression of people as either sympathetic, criminal, dangerous, or trustworthy.[2] This flipping between good and bad is expressed at both low and high levels of face processing. For example, we proceed and memorize differently faces of strangers previously introduced to us via a single short sentence as either norm violators (e.g., "forcibly raped a young woman") or benefactors (e.g., "donated $25,000 to cancer research"). It appears that we tend, somehow, to more readily dehumanize perpetrators and humanize (e.g., perceive more sentience or emotions in them) those described as nonnorm violators or benefactors.

A face can be detailed based on a catalogue of surface characteristics that are skin deep. Alternatively, it can be perceived as the mask that reveals or conceals ideas, beliefs and complex feelings, eyes and mouth becoming "windows to the soul." Surface face processing is the route to discriminating "bad people." Deep face processing, or mind reading, is the route we are more inclined to take for those we frame as good. We tend to personify and go deeper, hence humanize those we associate with good deeds. The reverse is true for those we immediately associate with bad deeds, inclined to perceive and approach them as hollow, mindless objects, dead shells on a beach.

Holistic (configural) processing as opposed to feature-based or piecemeal processing of the various parts of a face are two major kinds of face processing typically documented in the experimental literature. Research shows that the weight of these two kinds of processing varies systematically with the degree of familiarity and implicit trust detected in the face, this within a few milliseconds.[3]

When we are primed with positive stories about a face, we tend to process it more holistically, as a total configuration that is more than the sum of its parts. The reverse is true for faces that are either unfamiliar, from outgroup member, another race, or if primed with information on prior norm violations. Research shows that faces described as perpetrators, as in prison mug shots, tend to be remembered significantly more for their detailed features (fat lips, green eyes, crew cut). These faces are also less subject to the well-documented face inversion effect: the increase difficulty at recognizing people when their picture is inverted 180 degrees. Face inversion effect is a

[2] See the numerous works by Alexander Todorov and collaborators at Princeton University, for example, Willis, J., & Todorov, A. (2009). First impressions: Making up your mind after a 100-ms exposure to a face, *Psychological Science, 17*(7), 592–598.

[3] Todorov, A., Pakrashi, M., & Oosterhof, N. N. Evaluating faces on trustworthiness after minimal time exposure. *Social Cognition, 27*(6), 813–833.

well-known hurdle to typical whole face (holistic) processing with a dedicated piece of brain real estate to process such information (i.e., face fusiform area in the inferior temporal cortex).

In sum, research demonstrates that there are markedly different levels at which we perceive and infer characteristics in people. These levels vary in depth and complexity, affecting our memories, judgments, and social attitudes. What makes us invariably switch processing levels, from surface to deep and inversely, is familiarity and affiliation, whether the other is perceived as either proximal or distal in relation to our multiple categorical spheres of comfort and alliance: same versus different group, team, membership, family, cohort, gender, race, class—you name it—all the forced contrasts that make us think the world in black and white.

14

Fundamental Attribution Error

In a famous quote, social psychologist Fritz Heider (b. 1896–d. 1988) writes
that the behavior we witness in others tends to "engulf the total field."[1] By
the same token, he also writes: "To conceive of a person as having positive
and negative traits requires a more sophisticated view; it requires a differ-
entiation of the representation of the person into subparts that are of unlike
value."[2] Both of these remarks are very relevant to this book. I will review
them in turn.

The first quote means, in a nutshell, that when we see people behaving, we
are not just neutral observers of their behavior, but rather, we are quick to
infer causal explanation as to why people behave the way they do within the
totality of the situation they are "engulfed" or embedded in.

In a seminal 1944 experiment Heider did in collaboration with Marianne
Simmel,[3] they showed that we have an irresistible propensity to attribute
what we can call illusionary social causes. Heider and Simmel demonstrate
that adult participants viewing a series of simple animations involving plain
outlines of standard geometric objects like squares and triangles presented in
scratchy black and white movies were compelling enough for much obligatory meaning-making illusions. The participants report systematically seeing
the triangle as being "trapped" in an enclosure (a simple two-dimensional
outline), "wanting" to leave the enclosure, "trying" to open an exit door from
the enclosure, eventually perceived as being "helped," "rescued," or "intentionally" kept prisoner by a square. For Heider, this "engulfing of the total
field" gives rise to an automatic conflation of the movement dynamic of these
nondescript geometrical figures with folk psychology and our natural inclination to attribute social causes to any behaviors, even behaviors of the
most neutral and unlike any people we know. In other words, Heider and

---

[1] Heider, F. (1958). *The psychology of interpersonal relations*. New York, NY: Wiley, p. 54.
[2] Ibid., p. 182.
[3] Heider, F., & Simmel, M. (1944). An experimental study of apparent behavior. *American Journal of Psychology*, 57(2), 243–254.

Moral Acrobatics. Philippe Rochat, Oxford University Press (2021). © Oxford University Press.
DOI: 10.1093/oso/9780190057657.003.0014

Simmel demonstrated our natural inclination toward the implicit projection of spirits or mindness into things—what we call animism.

Of relevance to this book is the fact that our natural propensity to interpret behavior in terms of mentalist causal attribution is a key element and the foundation of much of our moral decisions regarding the right or wrong of people's behavior. In our moral judgments, we do invent motives behind actions.

Heider and Simmel's seminal study shows that we tend to be blindly misled in attributing necessary causal explanations in the same way that we are irresistibly inclined to attribute illusory mental states even to simple moving triangles or squares, so simple that they are not even wearing goggled eyes to simulate a person. That means that we are prone to make illusionary judgments and create attitudes for ourselves that are indeed linked to a perception that "engulfs the total field." This field becomes automatically a *moral* space, made of attitudes, mental states, and beliefs. Based on the abstract animations, Heider and Simmel's participants irresistibly created moral values in what they saw: "nasty" triangle, "helping" circle, "coward" square, etc.

In the 1950s and 1960s, another pioneer perception psychologist, Belgian Albert Michotte (b. 1881–d. 1965), demonstrated similar irresistible causal attributions to geometric figures "pushing" or "stopping," some inferred to be "heavier" than other, etc. Michotte[4] showed that we tend to directly infer causal links from our perceptions in compulsively trying to create meanings and make sense of them. In short, these seminal studies demonstrate that we are prone to jump the gun and see mental states where obviously there are none. We live in a world that is greatly imagined and made of quick and dirty inferences, especially in the social domain that is mined with moral heuristics and other quick moral judgments.

What is interesting is that both Heider and Michotte (but particularly Heider) were inspired by gestalt psychology, a theory claiming that we have innate (evolved) propensities to perceive organized wholes rather than simply the addition of discrete parts: "The whole we perceive is greater than the sum of the parts" is the theory's main motto. Gestalt psychologists ran numerous experiments showing that perceptual systems are attuned to basic principles that automatically organize and parse features in the total perceptual field. Heider did contribute to import the gestalt views into the social

---

[4] Michotte, A. (1946/1962). *The perception of causality*. Andover, MA: Methuen.

realm. For Heider and others, causal attribution principles in the social do-main mirrors what Gestalt psychologists describe in the realm of perception. There would be a direct analogy between the principles of organization that cause us to parse the perceived world of objects into discrete entities and the automatic parsing of causes and reasons underlying particular behaviors and social interactions. As we will see, it might also be the source of major moral blind spots or moral erroneous shortcuts, what we might also call moral pulls or "drifts" in the way we perceive and understand others.

A major moral drift is the so-called fundamental attribution error[5] or cor-respondence bias[6] that is now well documented and featured prominently in all introduction to psychology textbooks. This error consists in the pro-pensity to erroneously explain and attribute strongly biased causes to the behaviors of self and others. At least in our individualistic Western cultures, increasingly worldwide culture, where much emphasis is put on the indi-vidual rather than the group, we tend to make attribution and explain self as well as others' behavior mainly in terms of dispositional features of the individual and much less in terms of the situation in which the person is embedded (e.g., social class, economic resources, place in society, etc.). The latter tends to be viewed as somehow independent and unrelated to what a person is, despite the fact that, in reality, it does play a major causal role in shaping the life of the individual. Considerations for dispositional versus sit-uational factors are rarely balanced. This fact is true across cultures, some-times in inverse ways.[7]

In Western industrial and urban cultures, we tend to psychologize personal understanding, overlooking external factors like chance and accidents, mishaps, cultural or familial circumstances. As Heider was first to point out, we are strongly biased toward weighing individual "internal" dispositions as causes of particular behaviors but most importantly of how we construe individuals' destiny. This fundamental attribution error goes a long way in our moral decisions and attitudes toward others, how we con-strue relative responsibility, and how we explain how one gets to where he

---

[5] Ross, L. (1977).The intuitive psychologist and his shortcomings: Distortions in the attribution process. In L. Berkowitz (Ed.), *Advances in experimental social psychology* (Vol. 10, pp. 173–220). New York, NY: Academic Press.

[6] Fiske, S. T., & Taylor, S. E. (1991). *Social cognition* (2nd ed.). New York, NY: McGraw-Hill; Jones, E. E. (1979). The rocky road from acts to dispositions. *American Psychologist, 34,* 107–117; Jones, E. E. (1990). *Interpersonal perception.* New York, NY: Freeman.

[7] Nisbett, R. E., & Ross, I. (1980). *Human Inference: Strategies and shortcomings of social judgment.* Englewood Cliffs, NJ: Prentice-Hall.

is in life, overlooking situational factors like inherited social and economic circumstances. Indeed, we do not choose our family, and we inherit at birth a developmental niche, a product of a great roll of the dice. No one would contest, among other things, that this roll of the dice makes one's social climb more or less steep and slippery. Nonetheless, in our individualistic cultures, we tend to overweigh an individual's dispositions in our understanding of them and our judgments of their actions. This phenomenon is a major moral blind spot that seems to be universal, yet can go both ways.

In non-Western cultures, inversely, the group and the external situation can be strongly overweighed compared to dispositional factors, a reversed tendency and imbalanced judgmental and attitudinal propensity. For example, anthropologist Brad Shore,[8] an expert in Samoan (Polynesian) culture, recounts a story where one day he complained to his adoptive Samoan father that one of his brothers stole money from his wallet. In response, the father scolded the anthropologist, accusing him of having tempted his brother, creating inescapable envy by leaving his wallet unattended. Because of a profoundly different way of relating to one another, in a much more group-oriented, communal existence, the thief turns out to be the victim of temptations, a perspective that violates the typical Western individualistic perspective on possessions.

In Samoa, as in most non-Western group-oriented (collectivistic[9]) cultures, it is the community's responsibility to guide and prevent individuals from falling prey to their own selfish desires and other envies. Likewise, when a child misbehaves, disrupting the classroom, Japanese preschool teachers tend to perceive that the class as a group is faulty and doing something wrong, not able to integrate the problematic child into the collective. In the West we tend to attribute the cause of disruptive symptoms to the individual child, in some cases prescribing drugs and other one-on-one remediation. In Japan, these symptoms tend to be perceived as collective rather than individualistic.[10]

---

[8] Personal communication. For more thorough insights into Samoan values regarding ownership and property, see also Shore, B. (1982). *Sala'ilua: A Samoan mystery*. New York: Columbia University Press.

[9] Triandis, H. C; Gelfand, M. J. (1998). Converging measurement of horizontal and vertical individualism and collectivism. *Journal of Personality and Social Psychology, 74*(1), 118–128.

[10] Tobin, J.J., Wu, D.Y.H., Davidson, D.H. (1989). *Preschools in three cultures: Japan, China, and the United States*. New Haven: Yale University Press.

15

Clustering and Stereotyping

Overall, we are remarkably impressionistic and all-encompassing in our views of people, particularly when it comes down to our political views. We talk about the Chinese, the Americans, or the Arabs as if they were perfectly homogeneous groups of people in the millions, talking the same language and having similar collective dispositions, all of it because for more or less recent historical reasons, they are under the same national constitution. In fact, in all these countries there are marked cultural differences across provinces, regions, even valleys or villages, as we see in Switzerland. These differences are overlooked by outsiders, but highly relevant to natives. We are fundamentally coarse in our appreciations, judgments, and inferences, blinding ourselves of cultural distinctions and blind to all things that are most relevant to natives. Because of our ignorance and lack of experience, we tend to cluster together under one all-encompassing ethnic or national label: "the Arabs," "the Muslims," "the Chinese," "the Europeans," "the European Americans," "the African Americans."

The issue of national identity is particularly thorny in the context of recent mass immigration in Europe and elsewhere, confounding if you dig below the surface.[1] What is a European aside from having an EU passport and being confined within a larger economic region with a single currency? The question of national identity is barbed when what is shared is primarily economic convenience, peace among community members, and a large alliance motivated by competition against other large economic unions like the United States, China, or Russia. In the end, these national identity amalgams correspond to historical alliances and large-scale social organizations that protect collective comfort zones. They stand for political and economic status quo under the veneer of elusive essential values like religion, language, and selective cultural habitus: etiquettes, ways of dressing, eating, celebrating, and particular interactive rituals.

---

[1] On the topic of such embarrassment, see Descombes, V. (2013). *Les embarras de l'identité* [The embarrassment of identity]. Paris, France: Gallimard.

Moral Acrobatics. Philippe Rochat, Oxford University Press (2021). © Oxford University Press.
DOI: 10.1093/oso/9780190057657.003.0015

Social clustering and stereotyping are both unavoidable and necessary to navigate and try to make sense of the social world and yet also a source of major moral blind spots. It is part of the necessity to parse to predict, make decisions, and, ultimately, create meanings. This process leads to our natural inclination to cluster and create an information amalgam leading to much illusory correlations and biased attitudes in thinking about Blacks, Whites, Russians, Chinese, women, men, gays, straights, or Europeans as wholes having in common elusive essential characteristics. Social stereotypes have typically a negative connotation, linked to racism and all sorts of prejudices and discrimination toward minorities. However, they can be both negative and/or positive (e.g., Jews tend to be smart; Blacks are prone to be criminals). The ultimate function of social clustering and stereotypes is always to create contrasts that typically uphold one's own group advantage, ultimately in defense of one's own group sense of superiority and ascendance.

Social stereotypes do not just help us in thinking about the social world; they can also hinder how we perform as individuals and foresee obstacles for oneself. For example, the negative effects of gender and racial stereotypes related to minorities are abundantly documented under the umbrella term of *stereotype threat*. Stereotype threat corresponds to the phenomenon by which individuals who identify with a social group that have negative values attached to it are somehow irresistibly inclined to confirm them—the stereotypical notion that women are worse than men at math or that Blacks tend to have lower IQs than Whites.[2] The perception of these ill-founded notions can become self-fulfilling prophecies and paralyzing for individuals of these groups, hindering the actualization of their intellectual potential and a source of self-inflicted prejudices that, in return, reinforce ill-founded discriminatory assumptions. These assumptions rest on faulty generalizations and shortcut inferences regarding why, for example, women are a minority in science, technology, engineering, and mathematics (STEM) disciplines or why menial jobs are filled predominantly by Blacks. Even the most highly educated and cognizant individuals fall into these sorts of amalgam traps.

Larry Summers, ex-president of Harvard and, more recently, Nobel Prize laureate Tim Hunt, an honorary professor in biochemistry at the prestigious University College London, had to resign from their jobs because of sexist,

---

[2] Steele, C. M. (1997). A threat in the air: How stereotypes shape intellectual identity and performance. *American Psychologist, 52*(6), 613–629.

quick, and dirty assumptions they indulged in, in a public, loose moment.[3] Hunt declared on June 8, 2015 to a large audience at a world conference on science journalism in South Korea: "Let me tell you about my trouble with girls. Three things happen when they are in the lab: You fall in love with them, they fall in love with you, and when you criticize them they cry." Indulgent amalgam from the smartest, most educated guy imaginable, willing to generalize from local personal stories "with girls," to billions of women at large and millions involved in science labs around the world. Powerful, educated, and reputable individuals are not immune to moral blind spots. Our inclination toward damning amalgams defies education and other efforts toward political correctness. This inclination is deep and inescapable and tightly linked to how the mind works.

There is an abundance of research demonstrating our implicit attitude bias toward minorities, despite all of our declared, explicit efforts to be just and equitable toward them. Chicago police officers are shown to shoot systematically faster at Black protagonists compared to White protagonists depicted as fugitive criminals in shooting range videogames. Numerous other experimental studies show that White individuals of all classes tend to be significantly faster at associating negative adjectives (bad, sad, scary, stinky, etc.) with pictures of Black faces as opposed to White faces. Such implicit attitude and negative social biases toward Blacks do exist despite our strong explicit claim that we are not racist and that we toasted Obama as president. We have the natural tendency to create strong emotional categories based on faulty generalizations based on only apparent correlations and quick shortcuts. No one is immune to strong prejudices, a product of how the mind works.

Categorical amalgams are culturally supported and enhanced by all sorts of stereotypical accessories enhancing group boundaries, from uniforms including high-heel shoes, makeup, and dresses in the case of gender marking. Marking by way of uniforms and other external accessories objectifies and reinforces clustering and stereotypes. It objectifies and reinforces such processes by externalizing and making them visible. It also reinforces faulty generalizations. On the basis of such amalgams, values and judgments are quickly formed. Each era has its favorite accessories to mark social

[3] Summers, L. H. (2005, January 14). Remarks at NBER Conference on Diversifying the Science & Engineering Workforce. *Harvard University, Office of the President*. Retrieved from https://www.harvard.edu/president/speech/2005/remarks-nber-conference-on-diversifying-science-engineering-workforce; regarding Tim Hunt, see, for example, McKie, R. (2015, June 13). Shamed Nobel laureate Tim Hunt ruined by rush to judgment after stupid remarks. *The Guardian*. Retrieved from http://www.theguardian.com/science/2015/jun/13/tim-hunt-forced-to-resign.

distinction, from class to gender. Grotesque-looking wigs and dresses were the fashionable norm among the aristocrats in the era of Louis XIV. Towering high-top hats were worn with distinction by the 19th-century bourgeois males from New York to Berlin.

Stereotypes and associated biases are hard to shake, linked to the necessity to parse and cluster, the necessity to make sense by creating meaningful, albeit biased but helpful contrasts at all levels of mental processing, from perception (even sensation as we have seen) to cognition and meta-cognition. It is all about categorizing and creating conceptual amalgams upon which we can think and extrapolate about people and things—in short, to parse, to think, and to make decisions.

In the social and moral domains we think and extrapolate about our own situation in relation to others, creating value, first for ourselves and for those we identify with as extensions of our embodied self: family, friends, team, army, compatriots, or any other affiliations, sometime created on the fly depending on contexts and situations. Each particular alliance tends to form compartmentalized moral spheres, each dictating particular roles and attitudes: parent, child, friend, collaborator, teammate, citizen, etc. Most of the time, we are remarkably apt at juggling these spheres, transiting seamlessly from one to another without any collapsing, each remaining intact and well compartmentalized. But when these spheres collapse, the conflagration can be deadly, a conundrum famously played out in Robert Louis Stevenson novel *Dr. Jekyll & Mr. Hyde*. Within each sphere, an individual might play a different and highly contradictory role, like Hitler painting or petting his beloved dog, Mr. Hyde roaming the streets of London at night in feverish mischief mode.

Above it all, there is the need to feed the comfort zone and harmony within each of our various spherical alliances, adopting convenient perspectives in a moral space that is poked with blind spots. Such moral blind spots lead to blatantly ambiguous and hypocritical attitudes and decisions, like Hitler's outrage against those killing animals while sending millions to their death, a symptom of a weird moral arrangement, an uncanny moral bricolage that we all share, albeit at very different consequential scales.

The clustering leading to prejudices and moral shortcuts derives from the same process supporting normal thought processes in general, how the brain treats information via parsing, chunking, and the creation of conceptual amalgams, bootstrapping thoughts and representations. It is part of the same general process by which we create contrasts to individuate things and put them back together into categories from which we draw inferences and make predictions. In this process, and at all levels of brain processing, we enhance and create illusionary similarities between those things that we see as belonging to the same category. Inversely, we enhance and create illusionary contrasts between those that do not belong to it.

In the moral domain, this two-way contrast creation leads, as we have seen, to faulty correlations and stereotypes, both negative and positive. They are the source of moral hypocrisy and double standards, rigid righteousness and moral bricolage, each with their own idiosyncratic, often hard to fathom logic and internal consistency like Hitler's vegetarianism or the sudden endorsement of a radically different ideology for Machiavellian reasons, like strategically sabotaging rivals within one's own political party.

We all practice moral shortcuts and frame our decisions with moral montages assembled for our comfort, overlooking inconsistencies that are blatant for those negatively discriminated by it, such as women in relation to the discriminatory and ill-informed moral montages and attitudes of Larry Summers or Nobel laureate Tim Hunt.

At the heart of our moral montages are necessary illusions and blind spots we tend to overlook systematically and with apparent impunity. We fill them in to generate some internal consistencies, often rationally shaky and untenable from the outside, yet emotionally fitting and providing some evaluative unity for the self. Hitler did not feel awkward being a vegetarian. He lived his decision not to eat meat as ethically consistent within his totalitarian views, as Gandhi saw his kind of vegetarianism as an intrinsic part of his nonviolent ideology. The lived principle of treating animals with dignity can belong to very different moral montages with their own internal consistencies, implicitly obvious from within the individual, but nonobvious from the outside, particularly to out-group members. A view from the outside can easily poke holes in any of our moral montages. In the end, moral montages are always a shaky bricolage.

Gandhi, Mother Theresa, Martin Luther King, and Nelson Mandela, all prototypical moral figures, were also shrewd politicians and activists who had to make choices and compromises without collapsing under the weight of contradictions. Compartmentalizing and juggling standards are indeed central features of all our moral montages. They allow us to experience some unity in what we stand for, defining our perspective in moral space, to use philosopher Charles Taylor's vocabulary. It is also the source of much self-delusion that we see and live as outsiders, particularly when feeling victimized or ostracized. Self-delusion and shaky moral montages infused with blind spots and righteous inferences based on fundamental attribution errors and stereotyping are the costs of improving our navigation of the social world.

What makes our moral montages hang together despite shaky rationales and nonobvious internal consistencies is some affective glue: what we live as emotionally coherent. Reason never captures what we feel from the inside. Loving and heroically protecting my children through means that are violent and discriminatory bring together the polar opposite of what drives me in the first place (love and altruism) and what it takes to be generally mindful of others.

Mothers do not procrastinate in protecting their progenies, expressing love by killing, if necessary. Nothing is more natural, yet inconsistent and contradictory from a moral/ethical standpoint. How can one sustain living with love and hate as complementary, inseparable emotional entities without collapsing under the weight of the screaming contradiction in absolute (Kantian and positivist) logical terms? We are indeed always neither one nor the other, but both. The question is how do we, moral acrobats that we are, balance it all. What makes the glue of all of our contradictions, and in spite of all of our blatant, inescapable contradictions? What gives us a sense of moral self-unity? That is a fundamental, moral question from a psychological standpoint.

In relation to clustering and stereotyping, as we have seen, there are both centripetal and centrifugal forces at play: the force that enhances similarities within the members of a perceived cluster (centripetal force) and the force that enhances differences between in-group and out-group members (centrifugal force). One brings together; the other expels. One brings in and is inclusive; the other throws out and is exclusive. Both forces exist in their complementarity. They are co-defined, mutually functional, like figures are to a ground; maternal love holds the potential for protective violence. One always implies the other, and the question is how they interact as well as how they are arranged within our particular montages that we subjectively experience them as consistent at both implicit and explicit levels.

Sociological students of totalitarianism like Nazism, or any other collective violence leading to genocide and ethnic cleansing, show that at the group level the same sort of opposite forces is at play. On one hand, there is the centripetal force that tends to reinforce in-group member unity by enhancing similarities via not only stereotypical visibility like strict uniforms, attitudes, and mannerisms but also simple binary ideas regarding norms of what is right or wrong, arising, for example, from blind-sighted interpretations of the Bible by Christian crusaders or of the Quran by jihad fighters. Associated with it is the centrifugal force of excluding those who do not fit the rigid normative criteria of tolerated in-group membership. Across totalitarian regimes leading to genocides and other ethnic violence, there is always the dual process of internal and external repression, the centripetal obsession of preventing impurity within the group expressed in the paranoia of impure elements infesting the group and the centrifugal obsession of preventing impurity by expelling and destroying it via violent normative ostracism (e.g., Aryan race purity or any form of ethnic cleansing).[4]

All totalitarian regimes have indeed in common an obsession with both external and internal enemy infiltration that needs to be eradicated by all means, a genocide propensity found across cultures based on recorded history and continuing to occur around the world, from Rwanda, Serbia, Cambodia, Myanmar, to former Germany. The innocent individual culprit of being born or belonging to a minority out-group culture tends to be systematically ostracized, even at times eradicated by the millions.

[4] Semelin, J. (2005). *Purifier et détruire: usages politiques des massacres et genocides* [Purify and destroy: Political uses of massacres and genocides]. Paris, France: Editions du Seuil.

16

Pervasive Fetishism

We all have the propensity to materialize our elusive sense of belonging to others. We are pervasive social fetishists, creating physical placeholders of our social alliances by making them more tangible for self and for others. *To thing* and *thinging* are neologisms introduced here to capture this propensity for both in-group and out-group members: the propensity to objectify alliances, transforming them into something more fathomable and collectively shared, something that has visibility like a flag, a totem, a genealogical tree, a uniform, or etiquette or mannerisms like gang idiosyncratic tags or gestures. It is the transformative process of alliances into something physical, a particular form of reification or thing-making, that everybody can rally around and refer to in an animist and fetishist way. The alliance or misalliance becomes embodied, literally incarnated in a tangible sign or symbol standing for it. It can take the form of ritualistic gestures like the recent choreographed ways of killing by ISIL, beheading of prisoners dressed in orange outfits as a reminder of Guantanamo. Thinging and associated fetishisms are major reinforcing mechanisms of social clustering, stereotyping, and other social categorizing processes.

Thinging substantiates ideologies, as in flags and rituals, making them sensible and tangible. It provides material analog or renders visible virtual essence to group thoughts and attitudes. Ultimately, its function is to glue social categories and the sense of belonging together by literally fixating the alliance process into something externalized, objectified. Something material and public like a flag or a totem, serving as a constant identity reminder, whether it is to attract and consolidate in-group membership or, inversely, to exclude nonmembers. Passports, flags, allegiance sermons, uniforms, language and narratives, totemic landmarks, or food all stand and are perceived as tangible group identity markers with both centripetal and centrifugal functions attached to them. In other words, in the social realm, thinging is the basic process by which we compulsively objectify our alliances and how we mark our social distinction at both the individual and the group level.

Moral Acrobatics. Philippe Rochat, Oxford University Press (2021). © Oxford University Press.
DOI: 10.1093/oso/9780190057657.003.0016

Thinging is equivalent to what anthropologists capture when they account for animism (imputation of life to inanimate, physical things) in their ethnography of pre-industrial and pre-Christian custom cultures. However, collective superstitions and animism are not the purview of individuals of "primitive" and traditional ancient cultures. It continues to be pervasive across all cultures, a major trademark of human nature. In modern Japan, for example, ancestors' Shinto cult via bell ringing and smoke rituals is still widely practiced. Charms and other materialized superstitions by gamblers and other athletes continue to be prevalent. Profoundly emotional and affective in nature, thinging and *thingifying* are irresistible human propensities that override reason. It is a human way of life, expressed in all cultures, from religion, to gadget attachment, to the irresistible lust of material possession and the compulsive consumerism fueling rich industrial economies. It is part of a general process of value or worth creation that is deeply emotional and affective and often the main source of irrational fears, in particular the fear of losing control over possessions and other acquired privileges, from land to national citizenship. The fear of losing control over possessions has always been the typical source of social tensions and conflicts across cultures and in all history.[1]

Like animism and fetishism (i.e., "the worship of an inanimate object for its supposed magical powers"[2]), thinging is a two-way transfiguration of virtual ideas or representation into material objects and, vice versa, of material objects into ideas as in the case of compulsive consumerism. At a social and, ultimately, ethical level, it also pertains to how we tend to construe others as groups. It captures the way we perceive elusive essence as tangible characteristics, justifying the clustering of individuals into groups, a process that reinforces and is the source of stereotypes and shortcut moral reasoning.

Thinging, as a process, accounts for the moral blind spots that arise from our essentialist views on people and their grouping: the instinctive and probably innate propensity to infer that people and groups of people are made of immutable and constitutive features, nonobvious essences that are not visually seen by the eyes but that we render visible and tangible via *thinging*.

Inference is the process by which we derive logical conclusions from a particular set of premises—for example, the logical and necessarily true

---

[1] Rochat, P. (2015). *Origins of possession: Owning and sharing in development*. Cambridge, England: Cambridge University Press.
[2] Fetishism. (2020). *Lexico.com*. Retrieved from https://www.lexico.com/definition/fetishism.

conclusion that Socrates being a man should necessarily also die, knowing for a fact that all men must die. The mortality of Socrates is a logical and necessary true conclusion. Our inferences, however, are rarely so clear-cut and logical, leading to necessary and sufficient truth value. Most of the time, we tend to create truth-value in nonlogical yet pseudorational ways.

Through repeated observations of people behaviors (the "priors" in terms of Bayesian probability theory), we can't help but infer patterns, clustering and categorizing information, often based on quick shortcuts, weak correlations, and, in the end, wrong assumptions. This clustering, in turn, opens up new ways of thinking about people and things; it can change the whole field in which we are "engulfed" in our predictive reasoning about people and groups, following Fritz Heider's gestalt precepts discussed in Chapter 14 of this volume.

The fact is that it is common to experience drastic sudden changes in how we evaluate others, such changes often occurring because of one single event that might disrupt basic trust or be the source of a major unexpected discovery leading to disappointment. The inverse is also true. Following a single event, trust might be boosted, changing our views on a person in a flash. A gesture can contaminate the whole person's worth. From being heroic and beautiful, someone can be suddenly perceived as cowardly and ugly. From commanding Harvard president and admired Nobel laureate, one uttered word or comment can lead to a tidal change in inversed reputation.

Fragile we are in our reputation, especially when the individual is powerful and under tight public scrutiny. This is another expression of our moral blind spots: always engaged in filling in the gap, connecting the dots, creating compartmentalized clusters and stereotypes around elusive essential characteristics that define categorical membership. These clusters can be suddenly reversed, suddenly reorganized as a different whole that is always greater than the sum of its parts: from Dr. Jekyll to Mr. Hyde, or vice versa. Expectations around us are high, our reputation fragile, and we all know it too well as self-conscious creatures. But what is actually inferred from such clustering? The short answer is that it is further clustering and thinging of elusive essential characteristics.

In short, social clustering rests primarily on thinging and the inference of elusive essential characteristics defining all members of a cluster. Such an essentialist approach is determined by what our brain is primarily designed to be: a feeling system that sorts out and creates meanings to make predictions about people and things. Such basic processes entail obligatory heuristics and probabilistic inferences that end up filling in moral blind spots, the inference of nonobvious qualities that would be the constitutive stuff or the "thing" that—in our heads—defines the essence of both individuals and their grouping.

17

Ingrained Essentialism

We are compelled toward essentialism: the obligatory inference of illusive values and substances that we experience and represent as constitutive of things and people. Essentialism is ingrained in us and is an intrinsic part of human moral psychology. It underlies our shortcut moral decisions. It also accounts for our universal inclination toward animism and fetishism: the tendency to objectify, substantiate, and reify events in the process previously described as *thinging*.

We do have the obligatory tendency to infer and represent the essence of things: what ultimately constitutes these things and caused them to be. This inferential propensity pertains to nonobvious features that in our head make things intrinsically distinct. It is a basic mental reduction yielding the "gut feeling" values we attached to things, those bottom-line feelings that ultimately shape our judgments and attitudes: Hitler or Charles Manson as *essentially* mad and bad. These feelings frame further inferences and typically feed self-fulfilling prophesies.

Our social perceptions are indeed affectively charged with inferred values based on previous coarse clustering and generalization. This biased process is universal and a fundamental mechanism of human psychology and moral decision-making. No one escapes it, including renowned figures of Western philosophy like Arthur Schopenhauer (b. 1788–d. 1860) pondering about "essential" gender differences. Here is what Schopenhauer writes about women's psychology in contradistinction to men:

> She is intellectually short-sighted, for although her intuitive understanding quickly perceives what is near to her, on the other hand her circle of vision is limited and does not embrace anything that is remote; hence everything that is absent or past, or in the future, affects women in a less degree than men. This is why they have greater inclination for extravagance, which sometimes borders on madness. Women in their hearts think that men are

Moral Acrobatics. Philippe Rochat, Oxford University Press (2021). © Oxford University Press.
DOI: 10.1093/oso/9780190057657.003.0017

intended to earn money so that they may spend it, if possible during their husband's lifetime, but at any rate after his death.[1] (pp. 167–168)

Schopenhauer continues:

> It is because women's reasoning powers are weaker that they show more sympathy for the unfortunate than men, and consequently take a kindlier interest in them. On the other hand, women are inferior to men in matters of justice, honesty, and conscientiousness. Again, because their reasoning faculty is weak, things clearly visible and real, and belonging to the present, exercise a power over them which is rarely counteracted by abstract thoughts, fixed maxims, or firm resolutions, in general, by regard for the past and future or by consideration for what is absent and remote. Accordingly, they have the first and principal qualities of virtue, but they lack the secondary qualities which are often a necessary instrument in developing it. Women may be compared in this respect to an organism that has a liver but no gall-bladder.[2] (Feature article, pp. 1–2)

Schopenhauer is recognized as a major influence in the history of Western ideas, a must-read for all students of philosophy, yet he is certainly not immune to coarse generalizations leading to major moral blind spots. We reason around the illusory, all-encompassing essence we see into things and that we are compelled to interpret as "natural and primordial," hence the true axioms of further theorizing. But such truth is elusive at best, easier felt than articulated, and when articulated typically revealing major flaws. It borders and opens the door to superstition.

Following Susan Gelman, a major researcher of the phenomenon of essentialism in children,[3] the essence of things is what pertains to "an underlying reality or true nature, shared by members of a category, that one cannot observe directly but that gives an object its identity and is responsible for other similarities that category members share.[4]" She lists a few

---

[1] Arthur Schopenhauer (1880/2010). *On Women. The Essential Schopenhauer*. New York, NY: HarperCollins (pp. 165–178).
[2] Ibid.
[3] Gelman, S. (2003). *The essential child: Origins of essentialism in everyday thought*. New York, NY: Oxford University Press.
[4] Ibid., p. 8.

illustrative examples that nicely demonstrate how essentialism is pervasive in our lives, manifesting itself in all corners of our thinking and underlying much of our judgments and attitudes, likes and dislikes toward people and things. Essentialism is indeed a fundamental heuristic (explanatory) bias and memory place holder in human cognition across domains. It shows how essentialism is pervasive from politics to art, philosophy, and even science. It underlies our judgments of what is good or bad, authentic or not, true or untrue. Gelman's list shows how pervasive and consequential essentialism is in our value judgments and decisions regarding people and things. Here is a list of illustrative essentialism facts borrowed from Gelman.[5]

1. The president of Harvard recently suggested that the relative scarcity of women in "high-end" science and engineering professions is attributable in large part to male–female differences in intrinsic aptitude.[6]

2. In a nationally representative survey of Black and White Americans, most adults agreed with the statement, "Two people from the same race will always be more genetically similar to each other than two people from different races."[7]

3. Nearly half the U.S. population rejects evolutionary theory, finding it implausible that one species can transform into another.[8]

4. A recent study of heart transplant recipients found that over one third believed that they might take on qualities or personality characteristics of the person who had donated the heart.[9] One woman reported that she sensed her donor's "male energy" and "purer essence."[10]

5. It is estimated that roughly half of all adopted people search for a birth parent at some point in their lives.[11]

---

[5] Gelman, S. (2005, May). Essentialism in everyday thought. *Psychological Science Agenda*. Retrieved from https://www.apa.org/science/about/psa/2005/05/gelman.

[6] Summers, L. H. (2005, January 14). Remarks at NBER Conference on Diversifying the Science & Engineering Workforce. *Harvard University, Office of the President*. Retrieved from https://www.harvard.edu/president/speech/2005/remarks-nber-conference-on-diversifying-science-engineering-workforce.

[7] Jayaratne, T. (2001). *National sample of adults' beliefs about genetic bases to race and gender*. Unpublished raw data.

[8] Evans, E. M. (2001). Cognitive and contextual factors in the emergence of diverse belief systems: Creation versus evolution. *Cognitive Psychology, 42*, 217–266.

[9] Inspector, Y., Kutz, I., & David, D. (2004). Another person's heart: magical and rational thinking in the psychological adaptation to heart transplantation. *Israel Journal of Psychiatry and Related Sciences, 41*, 161–173.

[10] Sylvia, C., & Novak, W. (1997). *A change of heart*. Boston, MA: Little, Brown, pp. 107, 108.

[11] Müller, U., & Perry, B. (2001). Adopted persons' search for and contact with their birth parents I: Who searches and why? *Adoption Quarterly, 4*, 5–37.

6. People place higher value on authentic objects than exact copies (ranging from an original Picasso painting to Britney Spears's chewed-up gum).[12]

In view of these facts, but also many others, Gelman concludes:

Essentialism is the view that certain categories (e.g., women, racial groups, dinosaurs, original Picasso artwork) have an underlying reality or true nature that one cannot observe directly. Furthermore, this underlying reality (or "essence") is thought to give objects their identity, and to be responsible for similarities that category members share. Although there are serious problems with essentialism as a metaphysical doctrine . . . , recent psychological studies converge to suggest that essentialism is a reasoning heuristic that is readily available to both children and adults.

Research shows that we have indeed an early tendency to differentiate and categorize (cluster) things and people not only on the basis of obvious perceptual surface similarities (same shape, color, size, function), but also based on deeper essential inferences and beliefs. This would be part of what was introduced over 30 years ago as possibly an innate propensity toward "psychological essentialism."[13] Such essential inferences or beliefs do not have to be precisely represented or articulated but can be simply construed as a fundamental default mental short cut we instinctively operate by, what those who introduced the notion of psychological essentialism describe as a default "placeholder" helping us to think about and conceptualize about the world. It would help us in the memorizing of relevant features by chunking the world into coarse constitutive clusters.[14]

In other words, we have the well-documented default propensity to make sense of the world by not just taking it at face value (what we perceive); rather, we compelled to infer essential nonobvious features like causes and what we construe as defining characteristics of people and things, what would constitute their identity and categorical membership. Such a default

---

[12] Frazier, B. N., & Gelman, S. A. (2005, May). *Adults' ratings of different types of authentic objects.* Poster to be presented at the 2005 American Psychological Society Annual Convention, Los Angeles, CA.

[13] Medin, D. L., & Ortony, A. (1989). Psychological essentialism. In S. Vosniadou & A. Ortony (Eds.), *Similarity and analogical reasoning* (pp. 179–195). Cambridge, England: Cambridge University Press.

[14] Ibid.

process is automatic and devoid of critical thinking, leading to many faulty thoughts and other heuristic shortcuts that fill in our moral blind spots, while maintaining unwavering subjective coherence in relation to what we perceive and believe about both ourselves and others.

Closer scrutiny shows that these beliefs tend to be primarily convenient sorting devices, often arbitrary, based on erroneous as well as illusory assumptions and irrational gut feelings. The meaning and ground of what we are supposed to represent, with closer scrutiny, tend to be unscrupulous, quick, and convenient sorting shortcuts that give traction to our thoughts: the prediction of what should happen next. Essentialism feeds our previsions and decisions. It is how fundamentally the human mind works, constrained to infer essential features used as placeholders for further processing, the special products of our imagination. These imagined features are reified, treated, and experienced as real objects. These features are established and valued based on their probabilistic power, leading to gross spin-off heuristics and other moral blind spots.

In the life of the mind, pragmatic adaptation prevails. It is primarily agnostic of ethical values and doesn't really care about prejudices in the first place. It becomes an object of thoughts only after the fact. In the immediacy of perception, action, and swift decisions, our brain is fundamentally driven by shortcut bets on what is most probably going to happen next. Our morals and explicit sense of right and wrong form an "essential" veneer that we lay on top of such adaptive reality, trying to bring explicit coherence to it. This veneer is unique to our self-conscious species, our proneness toward guilt and embarrassment. Human self-consciousness is indeed the cornerstone of the human unique brand of symbolic morals that delineates what *ought* to happen and *ought* to be next, not just what *should* happen and what *should* be there next. The *should* is something our mind shares with the mind all other animals, not the *ought*.[15]

---

[15] Note that this issue is topic of much philosophical and evolutionary controversy; see, for example, De Waal, F. B. M. (2001). *Good natured*, Cambridge, MA: Harvard University Press, or the more recent target volume De Waal, F. B. M. (2009). *Primate and the philosophers: How morality evolved*. Princeton, NJ: Princeton University Press.

18

Essentialism and Prejudice

Above and beyond the brain's mechanical computing process, there is creation of affective values captured in constructs like good versus bad feelings
or, more specifically, feelings of certainty as opposed to uncertainty and trust
as opposed to distrust. Much of human psychology derives from these two
affective polarities. The same applies to other nonhuman animals but we, as
a species, added a significant symbolic spin to the affective polarities that underlie certainty and trust. Our feelings of certainty or trust, rather than being
strict experiential emanations of what our brain computes as happening now
and what is going to happen next, seem also to be irremediably imbued, if not
polluted, with essentialist beliefs.

Basic aspects of our subjective experience are strict emanations of our
brain's main adaptive function, which is to track invariance over change, to
sense what is currently happening and what is most likely going to happen
next. From such mechanical computing processes emanates particular subjective experiences that are by nature emotional with more or less painful
or pleasurable valence. These experiential emanations energize the process,
providing affective meanings to it.

Humans can't help but generalize in ways that are rarely, if ever, dictated
by reason and prudence. We jump quickly to confirmatory and reassuring
conclusions with a propensity to invent things in reference to worlds that
only exist in our minds. Rather than being just games of the imagination,
these inventions actually influence, often unbeknownst to us (subliminally),
our attitudes and actions in the real world, in particular our discriminatory
attitudes and actions toward people.

In our individual as well as collective imagination, not only do we cluster
and categorize people, we also are remarkably quick at casting umbrella
judgments. We do so by stereotyping, the process by which we cluster people
based on default, shortcut heuristic assumptions. These assumptions are typically the product of flawed correlations that crystalize over time, such as, for
example, the tendency to assume that all men are predators or better at math
or that the darker the skin of people, the poorer and the more threatening

Moral Acrobatics. Philippe Rochat, Oxford University Press (2021). © Oxford University Press.
DOI: 10.1093/oso/9780190057657.003.0018

they are, or the tendency to cluster vegetarians as nonviolent and environ-mentally conscious.

Etymologically, the term *stereotype* derives from the Greek *stereos* (solid) and *typos* (impression). Thus literally, stereotyping means clustering on the basis of solid or firm—hence, self-evident yet nonobvious—perceptions. It consists on solid impressions based on default, typically implicit beliefs that are products of our fertile symbolic imagination. Stereotyping is the direct mani-festation of our tendency to reconstruct the world in ways that makes it easier for us to navigate, anticipate, communicate, and affiliate with others by cre-ating common enemies, a major social glue that politicians know all too well.

Stereotyping is yet another way of talking about clustering and catego-rizing as fundamental cognitive mechanisms by which the brain works to form content representations (i.e., meanings) of what it senses and perceives. Prejudice, which tends to have a bad rap, captures the affective component (value) that emanates from stereotyping as a basic cognitive (clustering) mechanism. Prejudice can be either implicit or explicit, with stereotyping being mainly implicit or subliminal, a process we are not aware of in our obligatory clustering of things.

As already suggested in a previous chapter, clustering is a built-in, auto-matic brain-based propensity. It starts way upstream, a process already evi-dent at the periphery of our senses, when sensory transduction at the surface of our retinas are enhanced via filtering, amplification, and fill-in completion processes. In contrast, prejudice, as an analogous downstream process, can be explicit and challenged by others. Political discussions typically revolve around it. It pertains to gut, often irrational reactions that we try to dress with more or less convincing rationale, with dressing performed in commu-nication not only with others but also with ourselves.

In a literal sense, prejudice (i.e., *pre* [prior] and *judice* [judgment]) means judgment made in advance of actual facts with the negative connotation of rushed, premature judgments. Prejudice also stands for detrimental consequences occurring to someone in contempt of some recognized norms (e.g., a public lie becoming *prejudicial* to someone's reputation for which rep-aration can be sought). In short, the innate propensity to chunk, cluster, and categorize things corresponds with the propensity to reproduce patterns of reality that are constructed based on ready-made or default implicit beliefs (i.e., stereotyping).

By further analogy, in the history of the printing industry, stereotype came to stand for the matrix plate that in the printing process replaced the original document from which all duplicates are made. Likewise, in the realm of psychology, stereotypes are matrices perpetuating and reinforcing implicit thought patterns or shortcut inferences, more often than not based on faulty correlations (e.g., vegetarians *must be* nonviolent; to be gay, one *must be* perverted).

Stereotyping leads to prejudice (i.e., premature judgments), itself a source of prejudicial (negative or positive) acts of discrimination based on quick and arguably always disputable value judgments. Prejudice does refer to all of our unfounded beliefs and irrational, often negative attitudes toward others. Following Gordon Allport's original definition, prejudice corresponds to "feeling, favorable or unfavorable, toward a person or thing, prior to, or not based on, actual experience."[1]

On the basis of our implicit beliefs, we create affective values that are reinforced and quickly entrenched in us by repetition, becoming part of our gut reactions. Affective value creation and reinforcement are inseparable from the process of stereotyping, itself inseparable from our built-in propensity to cluster things and people.

But what is the relation between prejudice and essentialism? Essentialism is what appears to feed prejudice. Simply put, it is the default conceptual system that gives prejudice its impetus. The built-in default assumption that things and people have essential, nonobvious characteristics (definition of *essentialism*) allows for the immediate experience of favorable or unfavorable feelings toward people or things prior to or not based on actual experience. Essentialism as a built-in default propensity to infer essential characteristics in people and things is indeed the source of shortcuts, themselves feeding prejudice and moral blind spots.

Prejudice and moral blind spots derive primarily from abusive, if not erroneous inferences that are essentialist in nature. Macho attitudes toward women or favorable feelings toward a guru leading to blind obedience and conformity is fed by default essentialist assumptions—the inference, for example, that women are made inferior men or that the leader of a sect has intrinsic superior intelligence and wisdom. The propensity toward inferring essential characteristics pervades all of our thoughts and feelings about things and people. Our social attitudes and prejudices, be they positive or negative, are energized and find their origins in our inclination to infer nonobvious essences in things and people. In addition, such an inclination not

---

[1] Allport, G. (1979). *The nature of prejudice*. New York, NY: Perseus Books, p. 6.

only constrains the imaginary reconstruction of a reality that makes sense to us and has some coherence, but also points to uncanny incoherence, as in the case of Hitler's vegetarianism.

If essentialism feeds prejudice, prejudice in turn tends also to feed our essentialist default assumptions. Prejudice reinforces essentialist beliefs in what psychologists label "confirmatory bias."[2] Confirmatory bias is the wishful thinking typically associated with prejudice and also with disastrous discrimination linked to racism, ostracism, and other forms of collective violence as in the case of ethnic cleansing. Confirmatory biases are pervasive across psychological domains, from memory to problem-solving and theory building in general, but more important for us here, it is pervasive in how we judge people. We generate values and interpret evidence in ways that are partial to our beliefs, lured toward short-cut inferences and illusory correlations, which promote blind moral spots and double standards. Essentialism and prejudice appear to feed each other in a vicious circle, accounting for the rigid tendency of our judgments and the entrenchment of our social attitudes.

---

[2] Nickerson, Raymond S. (June 1998). Confirmation bias: A ubiquitous phenomenon in many guises. *Review of General Psychology, 2*(2): 175–220.

19

Group Essentialism

Group affiliation is typically objectified in physical things like uniforms, a flag, or family totems. These things stand for and are placeholders of our alliances. Other animals do have ways of communicating and discriminating relative alliances via scents or gestures. Dogs mark their territory by urinating. They check affiliations by constantly smelling each other. We humans add a significant notch to our ways of gauging affiliation, in particular our own experience of being part of a group.

The notch we add is symbolic. It takes us to creative spheres unknown to other animals, for better but also mainly for worse. It leads to symbolic *spin-offs* and out of hand, spiraling irrational conflicts that involve self-conscious constructs such as embodied notions of patriotism, duties, pride, justice, or revenge. These self-conscious constructs are embedded in particular emotions, resulting in a psychology that take us way beyond the instinctive and comparatively more straightforward, literal, and hence more predictable psychology of other animals.

As a case in point, as I am writing these lines, I overhear on the radio that two rival, heavily armed motorcycle gangs engaged in a deadly shoot out leaving 9 dead and 17 wounded. This happened on a Sunday afternoon, at a bar, in a nondescript mall of Waco, Texas, where hundreds of bikers rallied. The deadly fight was over territory control, a symbolic and totemic fight among middle-aged gang members. But more specifically, and as crazy as it might sound, the deadly brawl was about a simple symbolic insignia with the word "Texas" that members of a rival gang dared to stitch at the bottom of their biker's jacket. It was about one word made public and purely symbolic of the authority over a territory. Psychologically, it is about asserting in-group affiliation around shared group identity values somehow objectified in a totemic insignia: a five-letter word on a leather jacket that stands for in-group cohesion.

"These bikers die for their color," one journalist comments on TV. But bikers are not alone. Many human groups continue to die or make

Moral Acrobatics. Philippe Rochat, Oxford University Press (2021). © Oxford University Press.
DOI: 10.1093/oso/9780190057657.003.0019

life-changing decisions for a flag, an insignia, a totem, a word, or a verbal in-sult, as in the case of legendary French soccer player Zinedine Zidane.

"Son of a whore" (*fils de pute*) is the verbal insult that apparently led Zidane to blow his fuse in the last seconds of the 2006 soccer World Cup final that cost the French team a penalty kick and the cup. At the decisive final seconds of the game, Zidane could not help but responding to the verbal insult with a sudden and damning head butt toward the adverse team player. Although it cost France the loss of the 2006 soccer World Cup, Zidane never manifested regret because, somehow, it saved the honor of his im-mediate family. His family values were placed above and beyond his career and the disappointment of millions of passionate supporters. In subsequent interviews, questioned by journalists trying to make sense of his gesture, Zidane responded: "Do you think that during the last 50 seconds of my soccer career and with what was at stake I did it intentionally? I did it because I am first *a man.*"

Following the dramatic event, public polls showed continuous support for the French soccer idol. People resonated to the evoked insult to family values driving Zidane's epic reaction. Fans related to his pride, loyalty, and family al-legiance. In spite of the huge national deception, they easily picked up on this "essential" amalgam of loyalty values expressed by Zidane, which fundamen-tally defines him as a person in relation to his close biological in-group. But it does not have to be biological; it could have been his team or his country. The player stood by his values and reversed the accusation, defusing the respon-sibility of the fateful head butt toward the out-group malicious member who deliberately assaulted him with the fateful words.

These examples are illustrations of the unique, essentialist way we humans express social allegiances and probe alliances by reifying elusive concepts like courage, pride, and loyalty, invested in symbolic gestures or phys-ical objects. The spectacular drama of team competition, gang wars, and other intergroup conflicts represents an opportunity for players, fans, gang members, and other protagonists to express and assert essential characters of their in-group and reveal essential characters of the out-group. It is an op-portunity to probe alliances, for protagonists to emulate the extent to which they belong and merit membership to the group. In relation to the general process of creating in-group values, the Waco case represents an opportu-nity for group members to gauge their own and other in-group members' degree of allegiance to their "brotherhood." Ultimately, fights and competi-tion promote essentialist inferences of courage, heroism, and self-sacrifice to the group. It is a permanent form of group initiation and consolidation.

In all cultures, rituals exist as ready-made opportunities for such in-group value creation and the assertion of in-group allegiance, typically around suffering and the overcoming of fear, starting with widespread circumcision rituals and other painful rites of passage validating the merit of in-group belongingness. No other species engage in ritualistic circumcision of their young, nor invent hazing practices and other spectacular opportunities in competitive sports for the public display and contemplation of essential virtue characteristics like courage, allegiance, or heroism.

Essentialism applies to groups and intergroup relations. This is particularly evident in the kind of blind-spot inferences we tend to make regarding in-group as opposed to out-group intrinsic elusive characteristics, presumably inherent to race and national identity. Both are ready-made constructs, but with no objective biological or even sociohistorical "essential" features. Indeed, what defines a Black person or a Russian except for skin color, geographic birth, or a passport? Anything but the intrinsic characteristics we infer and amplify from such surface features, guiding us blindly toward categorical attitudes and short-cut moral decisions.

As another case in point, on June 26, 2015, Yassin Sahli, a jihadist militant of the Islamic State of Iraq and the Levant (ISIL) group, decapitated his boss at their factory in the Isere region of France. In a follow-up gruesome installation, the perpetrator pinned the victim's head to the fence of the factory surrounded by black Islamic State flags. He objectified the essential hate motive behind the individual killing, symbolically enlarged to the ideology of the group, which essentially rests on the fight against any nonbelievers, a display of determination and sacrificial allegiance to ISIS ideology, a display of group reduction to essential binary either/or categorical characteristics, namely, believers or nonbelievers of a particular dogma. Enemy of the dogma are demonized and dehumanized as part of its active eradication.

From the outside, the natural shortcut reaction toward such horrific events is to see behind them an absolute, unfathomable evil hand. It is demonizing and dehumanizing in reverse. Obviously at a different scale, both perspectives are associated with the same two-prong irresistible propensity to demonize and dehumanize. In reverse, and by reaction to the crime, it is the same process that enabled Yassin Sahli to perpetrate his horrific jihad. From both vantage points, there is the propensity to create monsters out of enemies, devoid of essential human characteristics and virtues to facilitate their eradication. Holding and juggling these two vantage points is the inescapable dilemma faced by family members, friends, and intimate affiliates of disclosed "monstrous" perpetrators like Yassin Sahli. They are constrained to reconcile these views, often facing enormous majority contempt.

In a follow-up interview with the wife of Yassin Sahli, she tries to give back some humanity and goodness to her husband, to provide her perspective on her husband. She brings to the balance her own intimate, presumably more knowledgeable perspective. Weighing a more balanced and less binary, black and white view, she portrays Sahli as a particularly gentle family man and husband, raising three young children together. Immediately following the news of her husband's crime, she tells journalists: "Me, I know him, we have a normal life, I hear people say that it is a terrorist act, but this is impossible. We just spent a normal night together and then he went to work, as usual." Sahli and his wife, on all accounts, formed a quiet and kind family. Follow-up interviews suggest that all of their neighbors liked them. Fellow worker Abdel Karim describes Sahli as "mysterious, but also somebody very calm. When talking to him, he answered with kindness. He was a false wolf. He was a *wolf disguised as a lamb*."[1] Dr. Jekyll and Mr. Hyde redux.

We are quick to infer demons in our out-group enemies and angels among our in-group peers. This is a universal propensity, the stem source of exaggerated and artificially constructed contrasts, shortcut prejudices, and other moral blind spots. We create simplistic coherence based on faulty correlations, assuming that if someone commits an atrocious crime, he must be atrocious all around. Again, it is hard for anybody to reconcile the fact that terrorists are perfectly capable of being good family members, devoted and loyal children toward their parents, loving mothers and fathers. It is difficult to reconcile the idea that Hitler was a vegetarian, an animal lover, and ardent hater of meat eaters. Difficult to reconcile the idea that demonized enemy groups share redeeming essential characteristics with us and our in-groups. We can't help but dissociate these characteristics to articulate them in absolute categorical black and white terms.

Individual as well as group essentialism share an analogous, irresistible propensity to dehumanize the enemy and exalt all of the humane virtues recognized in the in-group. It leads to an either/or clustering phenomenon with

---

[1] Translated transcript from Radio Tele Luxembourg; see also Vantighem, V. Attentat en Isère: Qui est Yassin Salhi, le suspect de l'attaque terroriste? *20 Minutes*. Retrieved from http://www.20minutes. fr/societe/1640451-20150626-attentat-isere-yassin-salhi-suspect.

flip-flopping polar inferences of deeper characteristics with either positive or negative absolute connotative values attached to them. The same polar inferences apply to how we construe ourselves as individuals, a perception that is also full of blind spots and the source of ingrained self-delusion as to who we think we are in "essence."

20

Self-Essentialism

In our mind, we are more than our breathing body. We are also what we represent and the narrative construction of who we represent, in particular who we wish to be. This construction corresponds to a complex representation that we constantly play out and convey to ourselves as well as to others. We pick, choose, and constantly edit characteristics to build and brand our self-image. Self-image is frozen in time and adapted to circumstances—whether it is to introduce ourselves to an intimate lover or in carefully concocting our résumé to get a job.

In the managerial process of self-representation, we create a static object of something (our self) that is, by definition, dynamic and constantly changing physically and psychologically. Our moods, emotions, feelings, appearances, and experiences are by definition always in transition and on the edge of becoming something else. This dynamic dimension of who we are is hard, if not impossible, to capture in words or in our imaginations, whether or not this imagination is shared with others.

All we do when construing who we are is *thinging* ourselves, in the same way that we engage in *thinging* what we perceive as our in-group or out-group. In analogous ways that we engage in group essentialism, we also engage in self-essentialism with corresponding prejudices, shortcuts, and other moral blind spots. The way we construe our self is for the most part delusional, from the way we perceive ourselves in mirrors to how we sense others perceive and evaluate us.

When we look at ourselves in a mirror, we see much more than meets the eyes, inferring what others might perceive in us. Self-consciousness is thus replete with essentialism turned inward and presumed to be either detected or undetected by others, as in the case of bluffs or white lies. We are impersonators of who we represent ourselves to be, not only for others but also for ourselves, always fearful of being debunked as impostors or fakes. We do care about our own reputation, the reputation of being consistent for self and for others in what we think, feel and do. In caring about our own

Moral Acrobatics. Philippe Rochat, Oxford University Press (2021). © Oxford University Press.
DOI: 10.1093/oso/9780190057657.003.0020

reputation, we do create values for ourselves in relation to others, but that is the source of much self-delusion.

The self, as experienced in the mirror reflection, is uncanny and most telling. Our own image reflected onto the polished surface of a mirror necessarily tends to be seen as the image of somebody else, not what we experience within that body reflected back to us. There is a necessary dissociation between what we are and what is represented by this reflection that we cannot help but seeing as another. There is an impossibility just to see in the mirror the reflection of our literal self, in the same way that we might see our shadow perfectly tracking our moves, being perfectly contingent and dynamically transformed as we move through varying light and space, when, for example, we move about under bright sunshine. Rather than such literal, perfectly contingent perception, we see the self *as another*.

What makes the self-experience in the mirror so uncanny is that what we experience is somebody, which happens to be the self, but seen by an audience that is self-inclusive: we are part of it. In other words, what is seen is not our embodied self, but rather our public self. This necessary bias attached to mirror self-experience is the product of yet another form of essentialism that is now turned toward the self.

Even with multiple mirrors surrounding the embodied self, in a dressing room, for example, what amounts to the visible self is captured as a summation of various views from different angles, hence the various possible public perspectives of others on the self. Looking at the self at the center of these various mirrors, we are de facto forced to represent the perspectives of a panoramic audience looking at us simultaneously from different angles. We inspect and successively create values related to each of these perspectives, determining for example what is our best angle. This process of self-representation consists in a summation of visible perspectival aspects of the self, always guided by inferential self-essentialism and valuation—the kind of nonobvious characteristics we try to put on display for others to contemplate and evaluate. Self-branding with others in mind and for imagined audiences, we are compelled to prime particular features of ourselves that, in our imagination, stand for essentials of who we are, such as essential rebelliousness in the pierced, tattooed punk with Mohawk haircut or as socially aligned with success, power, and ambition in the clean haircut businessman in his three-piece suited uniform. All essential characteristics projected to the public eye for evaluation via systematic self-image management and self-branding, notwithstanding much self-delusion.

Looking at myself in the mirror, rearranging my hair or putting on makeup is much more than a simple functional act. It is an essentialist and inferential process of self-evaluation from a public vantage point: Do I look good for others? Do I cause good or bad impressions? If bad, what can be done about it? How can I fix it? What essential character do I want to project or protect from an outside evaluation? Underlying such self-rumination and typical branding of particular features of the self that would stand for essential characteristics of who we are (i.e., self-essentialism), there is always much comparison and competition with the essential characteristics we likewise project and infer in others (i.e., group and other essentialism).

We compete for looks like no other animals do, actively engaged in actions intended not only to preserve and enhance reputation, but also to destroy and deliberately tarnish the reputation of others via gossiping and all the dirty politics that tend to be the main content of our exchanges with others. As for anything else, a reputation can be valuable only to the extent that it can be compared against the reputation of others, a typical source of envy, but also of dismissal and contempt. Here again, the figure–ground visual metaphor holds: a reputation exists only in relation to other reputations. Contrast and comparison are inseparable not only from competition and envy, but also from the cultivation of biased views toward others as competitors. From such competitive and comparison context derives the natural inclination to cultivate contempt as well as an inflated sense of superiority or inferiority toward others. It is also the context of blind infatuation and ideological rigidities found in guru phenomena and other social polarizations like the blind rooting for a sports team. All are equal sources of prejudice, duplicity, and other moral blind spots.

PART 4

DEVELOPMENT

What Are the Origins of Our Moral Decisions?

Self-essentialism, the concern for reputation, and all of our cover ups and other moral acrobatics are expressions of a self-conscious psychology, unique to our species and raising the question of its origins, both from an evolutionary and child development perspective.

In the final part that follows, the focus is on this *origins* question, trying to address what might be the psychological roots of our moral decisions. The following chapters are meant to give an overview of human self-conscious psychology from a developmental perspective. It includes the first manifestations of self-consciousness in development, including the emergence of lying and deception in children, but also the role of culture in filtering the expression of moral ambiguity and hypocrisy: a universal feature of human self-conscious psychology.

21

Self-Consciousness in Development

Contrary to what some early psychologists proposed, William James and in particular, we are not born in a blooming, buzzing, self–world confusion. We come to the world already equipped with an implicit sense of who we are in relation to the world. Newborns, for example, do not confound double touch from single touch. They root toward someone else's finger touching their cheek (single touch), much less when their own hand touches their cheek (double touch). The newborn does perceive that a single touch specifies an object external to self (e.g., someone else's finger) and that the double touch uniquely specifies themselves as differentiated entity among other entities, and healthy newborns make the distinction via their rooting response within 24 hours of their birth.[1]

Already by two months, babies display systematic self-defensive reactions to impending collisions with objects moving toward them. They tend to raise their arms, lean backward on their seat, and blink when a visual object expands looming toward their face. It shows that they experience themselves as substantial entities occupying space, a potential obstacle to other moving objects calling for preventive actions.[2] By four months, typical infants systematically reach with their hands for objects they see that are within their reach, much less or not at all when objects are ungraspable because they are too big or slightly out of reach.[3] An abundance of studies converge to show that infants from the first few weeks of life manifest of an implicit sense of their embodied self: the sense of their own body as differentiated (distinct), substantial (occupying space), agentive (source of effects in the world), and situated as an entity among other distinct entities. However, it takes some developmental time for infants and children to express an explicit and conceptual sense of themselves, for them to become a public object of recognition

---

[1] Rochat, P., & Hespos, S. J. (1997). Differential rooting response by neonates: Evidence for an early sense of self. *Infant and Child Development*, 6(3–4), 105–112.

[2] Ball, W., & Tronick, E. Z. (1971). Infant responses to impending collision: Optical and real. *Science*, 171(3973), 818–820.

[3] Rochat, P., Goubet, N., & Senders, S. J. (1999). To reach or not to reach? Perception of body effectivities by young infants. *Infant and Child Development*, 8, 129–148.

and evaluation ("Hey, that's me in the mirror. Look how ugly or beautiful I am"). This objectified sense of self emerges only by the end of the second year at a time when children begin to manifest symbolic competence, the ability to refer to things with arbitrary signs. In the case of mirror self-recognition, children indicate that what they perceive in the mirror is not another child looking at them, but themselves as seen from a third-person perspective: in other words, their public self. The mirror image is how anybody sees, recognizes, and eventually evaluates them. Discovering a mark on their face via the mirror, the child will not reach toward the specular image, but rather reach toward themselves to touch and get rid of the mark, often with coy smiles and embarrassment. We do the same when we notice a piece of spinach on one of our teeth after dinner with a first date. From this point on, self-awareness becomes much more than the implicit, minimal, and more or less direct (reflexive) self-experience, something we probably share with all other animals. It gives way to the development of a conceptual notion of the self as a *person*, an elusive notion that defines human self-consciousness, the exacerbated trait of our species.

The explicit sense of what's right or wrong, acceptable or not acceptable—hence, what we typically understand by morality—is rooted in self-consciousness as described here. Of importance is the fact that at one point in our development we begin to construe ourselves as characters perceived and evaluated by others. These characters are embodied in our actions and acted out in dispositions, beliefs, and thoughts. We become *persons* and, ultimately, *moral persons*. This development is the necessary prerequisite for the corollary development of lying and deception, the topic of the following chapter.

Let's note that the etymology of the word *person* comes from the Etruscan word *persona*, standing for "theater mask." Semantically thus, in the broadest sense, the meaning of a *person* is inseparable from some staging of the self or self-presentation (i.e., our social mask).[4] The concept of person is therefore inseparable from the idea of staging or the public presentation and management of the self as an entity that can be judged and evaluated both by self and by others. The concept relates to the notion of self as being accountable in relation to both self and others—literally, a self that has a reputation. Once again, note that reputation comes from the Latin word *putare*, meaning "to calculate" or *com-pute* (with calculation). As humans, we do develop

---

[4] See Goffman, E. (1959). *The presentation of self in everyday life*. New York, NY: Doubleday.

reputation regarding our person and, in particular, its worth in relation not only to others but also toward self.

By definition, children in their development become a person proper when they begin to construe themselves as an entity that is public in relation to others, who is not only entrusted with the capacity to judge and evaluate but also is accountable, entrusting others to judge and evaluate the self.

This is a major, uniquely human developmental turning point that all healthy children take by the end of their second year. It gives way to major social and cognitive development, including the ability to construe what's in the head of others, so-called theories of mind. In parallel, and as a necessary developmental corollary, it is also the beginning of the uniquely human career in lying and self-deception (see next chapter). This is, from the perspective of human psychological development, the necessary and sufficient stem source of moral ambiguity as discussed so far. It is the beginning of wishful thinking and pretend play, the work of the imagination let loose. Children begin to systematically simulate reality on the basis of made up speculations that feed back onto themselves to become somehow detached and independent of what is directly graspable to them, what is going on in front of their own eyes.

From being primarily literal in the here and now of perception and action, by the end of the second year children become symbolic proper. Language development explodes, with children adding new words to their vocabulary, up to 20 words per day, tying them together to form meaningful phrases and increasingly longer discourses following syntactic rules they pick up, generalize, and eventually internalize. All this happens at this developmental turning point, as children pass the threshold of the human symbolic gate.

Simulation, speculation, and, in general, the work of the imagination that emerges by the middle of the second year and feeds onto itself are characterized by a novel way of processing information, which is *recursive thinking*.

Parallel, and possibly the major basic operational (cognitive) cause leading to the development of symbolic (referential) and linguistic (syntactic) abilities, there is the capacity for recursive inferences. This capacity is particularly pronounced and a cognitive trademark in humans. It accounts for most of our self-conscious and moral psychology. It corresponds to the cognitive ability of repeating an inference in embedded clauses, as, for example, in the reflective abstraction, "I think that he thinks that they think that I think, etc." This recursive ability is equivalent to a bootstrapping of infinite mirror reflections inside the head of the individual for contemplation and objectification.

This emerging trait is directly linked to self-consciousness, the human trademark propensity to infer how other people feel about the self and how one feels about themself in relation to others. Presumably, it is based on such recursive capacity that children might begin to elaborate theories about the mental states of others (i.e., theories of mind)—whether others hold true or false beliefs, for example.

In relation to human self-conscious psychology and moral development, this recursive or reflective capacity happens to be quickly and irresistibly turned toward the self to figure out how others perceive us. But also turned toward others to better control their evaluation of us. The self-conscious human trait did not elude early theorists of evolution. Charles Darwin (b. 1809–d. 1882) is struck and puzzled by the unique and selective human crimsoning of the face, a region of the body that is most conspicuous to others. In his book *The Expression of the Emotions in Man and Animals*, he writes: "Blushing is the most peculiar and the most human of all expressions."[5] Observing blushing in his son from approximately three years of age and not prior, Darwin highlights the mental states that seem to induce human blushing:

> It is not the simple act of reflecting on our own appearance, but the thinking what others think of us, which excites a blush. In absolute solitude the most sensitive person would be quite indifferent about his appearance. We feel blame or disapprobation more acutely than approbation; and consequently depreciatory remarks or ridicule, whether of our appearance or conduct, causes us to blush much more readily than does praise.[6]

These observations capture something fundamental and distinctive about humans, a unique motivation behind their social cognition: the exacerbated quest for approbation and affiliation with others, as well as its necessary counterpart that is an unmatched fear of being rejected by others, an insatiable quest for social recognition, and the unique care for reputation. In human development, the self becomes eventually a cognized entity that is objectified and valued in reference to others, through their evaluative eyes and in anticipation of praise and criticism. The enormous energy we spend deliberately working on our self-presentation attests to this, including

[5] Darwin, C. (1872/1965). *The expression of the emotions in man and animals*. Chicago, IL: Chicago University Press, p. 309.
[6] Ibid., p. 325.

reputation-boosting moves; distinctive class manners (e.g., snobbism); body building, accessories, plastic surgery, and other systematic staging of the self for the public eye; and the self-packaging, self-advertising (e.g., résumé), and self-staging that sociologist Erving Goffman (b. 1922–d. 1982) described in his book *The Presentation of Self in Everyday Life*.[7]

The uniquely self-conscious psychology we evolved, and that each and every child develops is, by definition, recursive and referential, symbolic as opposed to literal. It refers to an objectified (represented and recognized), as well as evaluative sense of self, *not just for itself*, but primarily in reference to others.

What is specific to human self-conscious psychology is that it elevates the here and now of social perception and action to a represented realm of referential (symbolic), recursive and reflective thoughts and abstractions. As already mentioned, it leads toward systematic imagination and mental representation, the opening of the human mind's pretend and great simulacrum theater.

The capacity for recursive thoughts and reflective abstraction applies to all domains of cognition, yet it has particularly heavy experiential consequences in the realm of social cognition because it primarily refers to the self and self-reputation in particular.

Recursive thoughts do open the doors to shame and guilt as well as issues of moral identity and conscientiousness, not just the knowledge of what others have on their minds, what they are going to do next that is typically considered in theories of mind research. It opens doors to morality, shared agreements, and mutually binding *norms*. For example, it determines who should own what and why in the realm of possession. It transforms the minimal experience of possession and possessiveness that all animals experience, into the sense of property as a shared, mutually binding concept.[8]

The self as a person is a self that is *moral* and has a sense of its ethical stance and situation in relation to others, as well as to norms and standards, whether what he or she is doing or presenting of the self is right or wrong in relation to others, whether it transgresses or follows norms that are shared. It corresponds to the notion of a normative self, an entity that is constantly gauging its own situation and perspective in relation to norms, particularly social,

---

[7] Goffman, E. (1959). *The presentation of self in everyday life*. New York, NY: Doubleday.
[8] See Rochat, P. (2015). *Origins of possession: Owning and sharing in development*. Cambridge, England: Cambridge University Press.

moral, and ethical norms. In this sense, the personified self is more than just an object of thought; it is an object of evaluation (self-worth) in relation to others (others' worth) and particularly in relation to norms that are shared with others, including etiquette, aesthetics, or expected ways to behave and perform in society (i.e., in relation to others).

The basic prerequisite for the awareness of the self as a person is a sensitivity to norms, and this sensitivity also emerges by the middle of the second year. A large corpus of developmental studies document that during the second year and from the time children manifest self-recognition in mirrors as well as the use of personal pronouns and adjectives (me, mine, etc.), they also begin to manifest a sense of pride in work well done or in succeeding at resolving a problem.[9] They start to show empathy and act in ways recognized by others as prosocial. [10] Interestingly, they also notice abnormalities in objects, preferring intact over damaged, even slightly damaged things (e.g., a nondented over a dented cup).[11] They start to manifest surprise, concern, and disappointment when something is or gets broken, such as a doll losing its arm. As stated by child psychologist Jerome Kagan, "the central victories of the last half of the second year are (1) an appreciation of standards of proper behavior and (2) an awareness of one's actions, intentions, states, and competences."[12]

Kagan's conclusion regarding the cardinal social-cognitive achievements in the second year is based on empirical evidence demonstrating the robust emergence during this developmental period of behaviors like mastery smiles, directives to adults, and distress to an adult modeling a novel action (interpreted as expression of inadequacy feeling on the child's part), as well as the first emergence of self-descriptive utterances.

From this period on, children add to their ability to conceive themselves as objects of thought, the comparison of themselves as objects to others.

[9] Kagan, J. (1981). *The second year: The emergence of self-awareness.* Cambridge, MA: Harvard University Press; Lewis, M., Sullivan, M., Stanger, C., & Weiss, M. (1989). Self-development and self-conscious emotions. *Child Development, 60,* 146–156; Stipek, D., Recchia, S., & McClintic, S. (1992). *Self-evaluation in young children.* Chicago, IL: University of Chicago Press.

[10] Eisenberg, N., & Fabes, R. (1998). Prosocial development. In W. Damon (Ed.), *Handbook of child psychology: Vol. 3, Social, emotional, and personality development* (N. Eisenberg, Ed., 5th ed., pp. 710–778). New York, NY: Wiley; Zahn-Waxler, C., Radke-Yarrow, M., Wagner, E., & Chapman, M. (1992). Development of concern for others. *Developmental Psychology, 28,* 126–136.

[11] Dunn, J. (1987). The beginnings of moral understanding: Development in the second year. In J. Kagan & S. Lamb (Eds.), *The emergence of morality in young children* (pp. 91–111). Chicago, IL: Chicago University Press.

[12] Kagan, J. (1989). *Unstable ideas: Temperament, cognition and self.* Cambridge, MA: Harvard University Press, p. 236.

This comparison of the objectified self in relation to others, and in general in relation to social standards, entails awareness of an objectified self that is enduring over time and, hence, is accountable for the long range. The child must be able to reflect on the self not only as an object, but also as a permanent entity that is reminisced from the past and projected into the future, beyond the here and now of experience.

22

Self-Deception in Development

Children first lie to themselves before becoming proficient liars and manipulators of others' minds (see next chapter). Signs of self-deception are precocious, but infants indeed tend to be delusional regarding their basic competences, darting down slopes as they just start to walk, still very wobbly on their feet, or trying to climb over impossible obstacles as crawlers.[1] Reasons for the need of constant supervision and why toddlers are at physical risk of their own behavior are because they do not gauge dangers the way we do. It is also mainly because they are self-delusional about their own capacities. Infants and toddlers have the propensity to engage in actions and play that are often way beyond their competence: climbing a wall, lifting large stones, wrestling a big dog—actions that feed the funniest home video shows.

When toddlers start to speak in sentences and are asked by adults to talk about themselves, self-delusion is again evident, progressively masked with more balanced and cogent views about the self. With age, explicit self-description becomes progressively more tamed, with the fear of being debunked as an impostor, the fear of ridicule and the embarrassment of overboasting. It becomes increasingly self-conscious, so much that it tames the original propensity toward self-delusion at the level of action.

Here is, in large strokes, what child researchers observe.[2] With the vocabulary explosion, from the third year children begin to spontaneously self-refer, depicting themselves as owners ("That's mine"), agents ("I did it"), as well as performers ("I can do this"), with grammatical accuracy and precise uses of personal pronouns (I, me, mine). There are three main periods in the development of explicit (verbal) self-description: very early childhood (3- to 4-year-olds), early to middle childhood (5- to 7-year-olds), and middle to late childhood (8- to 11-year-olds).

---

[1] Adolph, K. (2008). Learning to move. *Current Directions in Psychological Science, 17*(3), 213–218.
[2] Harter, S. (1999). *The construction of the self: A developmental perspective*. New York, NY: Guildford Press.

Moral Acrobatics. Philippe Rochat, Oxford University Press (2021). © Oxford University Press.
DOI: 10.1093/oso/9780190057657.003.0022

Three- and four-year-olds' self-description is made essentially of highly concrete and compartmentalized (not yet articulated) representations of observable features (e.g., "I can count," "I know my ABC," "I live in a big house"). It consists of a taxonomic amalgam of physical ("I have curly hair"), performing ("I am very strong"), psychological ("I am happy"), and social attributes ("I have a lot of friends"). These attributes also revolve around possessions ("I have a doll and a brother") and preferences ("I love pizza and candies").

Self-attributes in the young child's description entail valuation, typically unrealistically positive self-representations.[3] Young children often allude to their own self-esteem via depicted potency and pretend enactments ("I am very strong. See? I can lift that chair!"). What is relevant here is that, once again, the early expression of self-worth appears more often than not exaggerated and inflated, at least by North American three- to four-year-old children growing up in a culture where parents tend to worry at any signs of self-deflation and excessive timidity in their child. Self-assertiveness (as opposed to respect, modesty, and self-effacement) is particularly valued and nurtured by parents and educators of Western middle-class children, compared, let's say, to non-Western, more traditional, and less urban cultures like villages in the South Pacific. The role of socializing agents is indeed important in early self-evaluative and self-esteem processes.[4]

From five years of age (early to middle childhood period), North American children continue in their tendency to inflate their own capacities and virtuosity, cataloging various self-attributed, typically exaggerated talents and competencies in the cognitive, social, or physical (athletic) domains. Compared to thee-year-olds, they begin nevertheless to show signs of forming representational sets combining multiple competencies (e.g., "I am good at school, . . . at riding my bike . . . at having friends," etc.). Another trend in five-year-olds is their new propensity to present opposite characteristics about the self: "I am good at that, but bad at this." Such progress is described by researchers as children's growing general ability to map representations onto one another, here expressed in opposite sets.

In a third and final period emphasized by researchers, eight-year-olds and older children begin to form higher-order concepts in their self-description,

---

[3] Ibid.

[4] Higgins, E. T. (1991). Development of self-regulatory and self-evaluative processes: Costs, benefits, and tradeoffs. In M. R. Gunnar & L. A. Sroufe (Eds.), *Self processes and development: The Minnesota Symposia on Child Development* (Vol. 23, pp. 1125–1166). Hillsdale, NJ: Erlbaum.

including more global evaluations of the self and its worth as a person. Children might depict themselves as "smart," a trait acknowledged and understood by the child as encompassing many different skills, including interpersonal, academic, or athletic skills. Children from this age on do tend also to consider in their self-description that they are made of positive and negative attributes that *coexist* in determining what is relevant to the self. In other words, beyond a mere amalgam of catalogued traits, children integrate in their self-description the opposition of identifiable characteristics— for example: "I can be happy but also sad . . . do good things but also bad things . . . obey but sometime also disobey." With such integration of opposites, the child becomes less black or white, all or nothing, in his or her explicit grasping of selfhood, obviously an important cognitive but also emotional and socio-affective step in development. As already stated, by eight years of age children begin to show a more balanced view in self-description, a tendency that expresses an overall progress in taking an ethical stance toward the self in relation to others as evaluators.

In short, it appears that children become more relativist and measured in their self-depiction, developing a construal of the self that is morally personified (see previous discussion), with a sense of shame, pride, or potential guilt, combining strengths and weaknesses in relation to socially shared standards. Reflected in the development of self-description in children, social norms are progressively internalized, not only as a function of social experience and social adaptation; the experience of communing with family, teachers, and peers; conflicts and rivalry with parents and siblings; but also in the creation of new relationships and social alliances outside of the family.[5] We can assume that it is primarily from this experiential context that children develop self-identification or *categorical self-concept* as previously defined.

The social life of children is made up of novel attachments, intimacy, and self-defining social affiliation, beyond the first family bonding or attachment to primary caretaker(s).[6] But it is also a life made of conflicts, prejudices, and fears, particularly the fear of being rejected and not recognized by others.[7] In this context, *self-assertion*, or the need to affirm and make room for self in

[5] Dunn, J. (1987). The beginnings of moral understanding: Development in the second year. In J. Kagan & S. Lamb (Eds.), *The emergence of morality in young children* (pp. 91–111). Chicago, IL: Chicago University Press.

[6] Bowlby, J. (1969/1982). *Attachment and loss.* New York, NY: Basic Books.

[7] Rochat, P. (2009). *Others in mind: Social origins of self-consciousness.* New York, NY: Cambridge University Press.

relation to others, plays a central role in shaping and driving self-concept development. It is also the source of budding self-deception.

In an intriguing study performed some years ago, researchers asked a sample of over 500 U.S. third- to sixth-graders (8- to 11-year-olds) to fill in a 16-item self-report questionnaire assessing their subjective experience of *loneliness* and social dissatisfaction.[8] On a 5-point scale, children were asked to assess the relative truth of statements such as "I am lonely" or "I feel left out of things." The authors found that over 10% of all children, independently of age or sex, reported strong feelings of loneliness and social dissatisfaction. Validating this self-assessment, the reported feelings of loneliness and social dissatisfaction were significantly correlated with the sociometric status of the child based on peer assessment.

This study shows how much self-conceptualizing in children, particularly its content, depends on perceived popularity and peer recognition. It also shows how self-conceptualizing in development is more than a cognitive exercise: it often involves the objectification of social strengths and fragilities, the relative situation of the self in relation to others.

Self-conceptualizing is indeed primarily the process by which we situate ourselves in relation to others: how close or how estranged we are in relation to them, what impact and power we have on others. In this respect, children show us that conceiving ourselves might serve a primary social function: the function of asserting who we are in relation to others, an important process by which we capture identifiable characteristics that shape our behaviors, intentions, and social decisions.

Early on, and from the time children are able to objectify themselves as persons, the content of these identifiable characteristics (what they are ontologically) is mainly determined by how they compare to the perceived and represented (belief) characteristics of others. This is evidenced by the inseparable development of self-conceptualizing and the early formation of gender identity and social prejudice, the way children construe their relative *affiliation* to particular others by ways of self-inclusion and group identification, as well as by social exclusion: the necessary counterpart of any social identification, affiliation, or alliance.[9]

---

[8] Asher, S. R., Hymel, S., & Renshaw, P. D. (1984). Loneliness in Children. *Child Development, 55*, 1456–1464.
[9] Dunn, "The Beginnings of Moral Understanding." Nesdale, D., Maass, A., Durkin, K., & Griffiths, J. (2005). Group norms, threat, and children's racial prejudice. *Child Development, 76*(3), 652–663.

In relation to social prejudice, research investigating children's social identity development suggests that if from the third year children are explicit about their gender identity, it is only by age four to five years that they manifest an awareness of their own ethnic and racial identity. They begin to show identification and preference for their own ethnic group. They are also aware of the relative status of social groups they might or might not belong to, preferring affiliation with majority (e.g., White) rather than minority groups (e.g., Latino or African-American).

Early on, children derive self-esteem and, hence, a conception of self-worth from group membership and group status. Ethnic and racial preference manifested by five-year-olds is based on a drive to assert their own in-group affiliation and not yet focusing on the characteristics of out-group members that they would eventually discriminate or exclude.[10] Social prejudices, whereby some children might find self-assertiveness in focusing on negative aspects of out-group members, are manifested in development beyond the early ethnic preference phase of young children, no earlier than seven to eight years of age based on Nesdale's research and interpretation.

From seven years of age, children's sense of social affiliation determines their self-identification in relation to others. The norms of the group they feel affiliated with lead them to apply particular rules of inclusion or exclusion that determine stereotyped judgments and attitudes toward others. These include ethnic and racial prejudices that are shown to be exacerbated in situations of competition or threat from an out-group.[11] From this age on, the social dynamic of group affiliation plays a significant role in how children conceive of themselves in relation to others, particularly in relation to a selected group of individuals they identify with. In a complementary way, they also begin to specify themselves by *disassociation* with out-group members, expressing prejudices and attitudes of exclusion toward them.[12]

From seven years on, the self and social identity begin to be conceptualized on the basis of combined social affiliation and exclusion processes. In relation to self-delusion in development, these combined processes are contrasting or "bringing out" the self positively by association with some persons and

---

[10] Nesdale, D. (1999). Developmental changes in children's ethnic preferences and social cognitions. *Journal of Applied Developmental Psychology, 20,* 501–519; Nesdale, D. (2004). Social identity processes and children's ethnic prejudice. In M. Bennett & F. Sani (Eds.), *The development of the social self* (pp. 219–246). London, England: Psychology Press.

[11] Nesdale, D., Maass, A., Durkin, K., & Griffiths, J. (2005). Group norms, threat, and children's racial prejudice. *Child Development, 76*(3), 652–663.

[12] Ibid.

negatively by dissociation with others. From then on, children are subject to group norm influences. They begin to construe their own person through the looking glass of the group they affiliate with, as well as the members of other groups they exclude. In this dual (complementary) process, combining affiliation and contrast or opposition to selected others, children manifest new ways of asserting and specifying who they are as persons, their inflated worth of themselves as opposed to ostracized others.

In summary, social psychology research on identity development, particularly the origins of social prejudice and attitudes, reveals an important aspect of self-conceptualizing in development. This aspect is the process by which children eventually establish and assess their own situation and value in relation to others by combined affiliation and rejection, affiliation with those who give the child inflated self-values by contrast to ostracized deflated others.

Self-esteem or the construal of self-worth depends on such a process. It is an eminently social process that plays a major part in self-concept development from the time children start to conceive of themselves as *persons*, from the time the self is measured against social norms and standards, when children begin to conceive of themselves as moral agents among other moral agents. It is also the source of marked self-deception and delusion.

23

Lying and Deception in Development

Deception is pervasive in nature. Animals of all kinds raise their hair or feathers to appear bigger and thus evolved such responses to impress by faking apparent strength in the face of threats or a fight. Chimpanzees and other nonhuman primates join a chorus in loud hooting and screaming to show strength toward potential predators or enemies. Butterflies are designed to simulate large eyes on their wings and octopuses are equipped to fuse with rocks in camouflage. Evolved traits to trick other species and avoid predation abound among avian, fish, mammalian, and even invertebrate species like the hermit crab.

Pretense in play is not a uniquely human trait. Young and old nonhuman social animals spend a good amount of time engaging in activities that appear to have no other function than self-entertainment and the creation of intense, pleasurable sensations. Dogs play and engage in roughhousing just as children do. They simulate pseudo fights, big dogs tolerating the pretend growling and attacks of much smaller dogs, clearly suspending their original meanings. Not only dogs and cats but also wolves, dolphins, and birds unquestionably engage in some forms of pretend play. So what might be different in the human pretend play accompanying self-consciousness and the symbolic function expressed by children from the middle of the second year? It is *serious pretense* developing in parallel to the ludic (playful) pretense we see in other animals. Serious pretense pertains to deliberate deception toward both self and others. In other words, it is lies and lying, a special kind of deception unlike any other found in nature.

Human self-consciousness and symbolic functioning bring deception to new levels, incomparable to all the other forms of deception found in other animals, and in nature in general. It brings intention and open-ended delusional redescription of reality to fit our social needs, boost our self-worth, and maintain semblance of self-unity. Again, it is linked to our evolved ability to engage in recursive inferences: the cognitive ability of repeating an inference in embedded clauses, as, for example, in the reflective abstraction "I think that he thinks that they think that I think, etc." This ability leads us

Moral Acrobatics. Philippe Rochat, Oxford University Press (2021). © Oxford University Press.
DOI: 10.1093/oso/9780190057657.003.0023

toward symbolic, referential, and metaphorical representations of reality to fit our basic needs of social affiliation within our own spheres of alliance and zones of comfort.

But why and how do kids start to engage in delusional redescription of reality, tricking others to fit their need of social recognition and affiliation? Bluntly stated, when, why, and how do children start to lie? What are the origins of the human career in lying and intentional deception?

The development of recursive thinking, symbolic, referential functioning, and, in general, the infinite "bootstrapping" work of the human imagination does indeed bring deception to levels unmatched in nature. Human imagination gives way to a unique sophistication in tricking others, the ability and propensity to build sophisticated Trojan horses and other strategic decoys based on complex indirect and delayed deception planning.

This sophistication rests not only on recursive thinking and symbolic functioning, but also on memory and the ability to theorize about the mind of others, in particular the ability to construe and represent that others can hold false beliefs about reality, a precondition for them to be tricked the human way.

With the emergence of explicit theories of mind between four and five years, children begin to infer successfully what people are going to do next based on their beliefs, whether those are true or false. They will, for example, understand that people look for an object at the location they think this object should be, although the child knows that in reality it is at different location.

Across cultures,[1] the child becomes explicitly capable of contemplating both their own and another person's perspective, even when they contradict each other that, for example, others hold false beliefs or assumptions about the world. Children become capable of suspending their own knowledge to construe the knowledge of others, which is sometime false. This suspension and dual (perspectival) contemplation of reality is the basic, necessary competence, not only to infer what people will do next, but also for someone to *trick* others, and, a fortiori, the capacity to lie the way we do: deliberately and strategically, not by accident. An unintentional lie is indeed an oxymoron, a term's contradiction.

---

[1] Callaghan, T., Rochat, P., Lillard, A., Claux, M. L., Odden, H., Itakura, S., . . . Singh, S. (2005). Synchrony in the onset of mental-state reasoning: Evidence from five cultures. *Psychological Science*, 16(5), 378–384.

The perception of intentionality in others, whether, for example, their actions are deliberate as opposed to accidental or the construal of goal orientation in others is actually a very early fact of life, expressed in infants as young as six months.[2] Recent studies even suggest that by 15 months, infants look surprised, gazing significantly more at a person reaching for an object this person had no way to know it was there.[3] They react with enhanced curiosity, demonstrating an implicit understanding of false belief. Infants' reaction of surprise demonstrates an implicit understanding that where the person reaches defies what they actually know, a knowledge established based on previous exposure to where the person saw the object being hidden, then surreptitiously hidden at a different place. Again, the infant reacts to the fact that the person reaches for the object at a location she should not know, demonstrating an early implicit understanding that people can hold false beliefs, an acid test of the existence of so-called theories of mind.

It appears that the long-held idea proposing that theories of mind are the exclusive domain of humans is now debunk. Three great apes species, among our closest evolutionary relatives (common chimpanzees, bonobos, and gorillas) are now shown to have some understanding that others can hold false beliefs, guiding their prediction as to what the person will do next. However, what is special about human false belief understanding and theories of others' minds is our sophisticated use of such understanding to trick, deceive, and mock people, not just to predict what they are going to do next.

Humans put false belief understanding and theories of mind to work with unmatched degrees of maliciousness. It is the source of our uncanny sense of humor more often than not at the expense of some (e.g., Polish jokes) but can also be self-deprecating (e.g., Woody Allen). Intentionally, whether we want it or not, we constantly spread false beliefs in the heads of others in multiple, more or less benign ways: boasting, exaggerating, concealing, deflating, displacing, distracting, or down right lying by deliberately planting false beliefs in the heads of others. The spreading of false beliefs to gain affiliation and compete with others is what we do as part of a symbolic and theorizing (metaphorical) species.

---

[2] Woodward, A. L. (2013). Infant foundations of intentional understanding. In M. R. Banaji & S. A. Gelman (Eds.), *Navigating the social world: A developmental perspective* (pp.75–80). New York, NY: Oxford University Press.
[3] Onishi, K. H., & Baillargeon, R. (2005). Do 15 month-old infants understand false beliefs? *Science, 308*(5719), 255–258.

Aside from logical necessities like 2 + 2 makes 4 and other truths lived by us as absolute, like the probability that the sun will rise and fall tomorrow like it did today, truth does not dominate our shared mental world. More often than not, truth is negotiated, only approximated, and never exhausted. Religious truths experienced as absolute by believers, even of the same denomination, are endlessly negotiated and interpreted in theological debates fueling the worse recurring wars in recorded history of mass invasion, conversion (crusades), and extermination (religious genocides). Even in the hard sciences truth is based on probability. It is therefore impossible to survive socially without some ability to doubt and dispute the truth spreads by others, notwithstanding to spin and convince others of what we hold as true. In short, the human propensity to lie and deceive is a natural and necessary propensity children express from the time they reach the threshold of the symbolic gate. They enter a world that is not anymore just literal, in the here and now of perception and action, but a world of semblances that need to be appraised, negotiated with others, and used to survive socially. Children learn and develop quickly the ability to use semblances as the primary tool in their navigation of the social world, gaining affiliation through the debunking and deliberate creation of *false* or *pseudo beliefs*.

As symbolic creatures, we live in a world of pseudo truths. Lying as well as detecting lies is an absolute necessity for our own social survival. The human capacity to generate and deal with lies is on a par with the big eyes on butterflies' wings, the necessary decoys evolved for their survival. Deliberate lying, deception, and the fake representation of truth, from makeup for the enlargement of eyes and lips, to placarding medals like a large pancake on the bombastic chest of the proud 19th-century Russian dignitary in Figure 23.1. The range of human decoys is endless, often grotesque, if not pathetic. It is inscribed in the ultimate evolutionary logic of creating values for ourselves, and those we identify with: family, friends, institution, ethnicity, religion, nation, team, gender, you name it. It is also with semblances and often lies that we manage our reputation. Children understand this and develop their lying ability very early on.

The development of theories of mind and folk psychology—what's happening in other people's minds not only how to predict their behavior, but also how to manipulate their evaluation of the self—starts already in the first year at an implicit pragmatic level. Young infants, from their second month and with the emergence of first socially elicited smiling (as opposed to the reflex smiles of a newborn) engage in face-to-face proto conversations with

Figure 23.1 Portrait of a Russian prince.
Musée national de la Légion d'honneur, Paris.

others, attuned to their attention and degree of attunement toward the self. If the other person surreptitiously freezes in the middle of the exchange, the infant will start to disengage, self-comfort, drool, and eventually cry. This is a very robust and well-documented "still face" phenomenon found in all healthy developing infants across cultures.[4] Early on, infants learn and are

[4] Tronick, E., Als, H., Adamson, L. B., Wise, S., & Brazelton, T. B. (1978). The infant's response to entrapment between contradictory messages in face to face interaction. *Journal of the American Academy of Child Psychiatry*, 17, 1–13; Rochat, P., & Striano, T. (1999). Social cognitive development in the first year. In P. Rochat (Ed.), *Early Social Cognition* (pp. 3–34). Mahwah, NJ: Erlbaum; Broesch, T., Rochat, P., Olah, K., Broesch, J., & Henrich, J. (2016). Similarities and differences in

attuned to the pragmatics of interpersonal exchanges. They expect people
to react in certain ways to their bids of positive affect, by smiling back and
keeping eye contact. Already by two to three months, infants develop particular expectations that are tailored to the interactive style of their mothers.
Infants used to a highly responsive mother will prefer to interact with
strangers who are equally responsive. Inversely, infants of low responsive
mothers will tend to prefer low responding over high responding social partners.[5] Infants, from two months of age, and probably earlier based on smells,
handling, and skin contacts, develop their own zone of interpersonal comfort. This zone becomes quickly normative and selective. It contributes early
on to shape children's social preferences.

From this early selectivity and social expectations based on style and the
pragmatics of interpersonal exchanges, infants begin their career as mind the-
orizer and simulator, inferring nonobvious mental states that guide people's
actions: their wants, their hidden desires, their beliefs, or the emotions they
might hide. Infants develop an ability to go beyond a skin deep, surface anal-
ysis of others' behaviors in relation to them. This ability develops markedly
from the middle of the second year with the expression of implicit theories of
mind and false belief understanding.

By the middle of the second year infants show surprise when someone
reaches toward a hidden object at a location they were not supposed to
know.[6] From this age on, infants do infer wants and particular desires guiding
choices and actions in others. They do not use words yet to describe their
construal of others' minds, but they behave accordingly. They reveal mind
reading at the implicit level of their responses guided by particular expectations they infer from seeing others and interacting with them. By the end of
the second year, and even prior, their folk psychology is more than skin deep.

Before their first birthday, infants do pick up on the features of intentional as opposed to accidental actions in others. They do make the distinction between planned and unplanned actions, inferring a mind behind the
former. For example, infants will be surprised, looking longer at a real hand

maternal responsiveness in three societies: Evidence from Fiji, Kenya and US. *Child Development,*
87(3):700–711.

[5] Bigelow, A., & Rochat, P. (2006). Two-month-old infants' sensitivity to social contingency in
mother-infant and stranger–infant interaction. *Infancy,* 9(3), 313–325.
[6] Onishi, K. H., & Baillargeon, R. (2005). Do 15-month-old infants understand false beliefs?
Science, 35(308), 255–258.

reaching toward a wrong location and, in contrast, they will be comparatively unphased if the hand is artificial like a plyer or a pincer.[7]

The mind that children infer in others at both implicit (prelinguistic) and explicit (linguistic) levels develops rapidly from simple to increasingly interpretative and speculative levels, from the early construal of persons' wants and desires (that someone wants to interact with me, likes or dislikes me, likes or dislikes broccoli), to an actual representation or construal of others' beliefs proper (what a person thinks that I think that she thinks, etc.). This is a huge step that has many ramifications in how children relate to others.

For child development researchers, albeit not all of them, this represents a major conceptual change that is linked to the growing referential and symbolic competence of the child in representing and simulating the world around, including people, beyond the here and now of perception and action.

By three years of age, children understand that seeing is knowing, that if someone lays her eyes on an object, picks it up, and memorizes its location, that she expects to find it there a minute later. Yet what the child understands is that the person has a "copy" (true) representation of the object she saw at that particular location, which corresponds to what the child knows. If the object is displaced or transformed unbeknownst to the person, the child will have a hard time explicitly talking about and representing that she will now hold a false belief about the object and its location. It takes some developmental time for children to dissociate their own from others' knowledge about things, a crucial step toward the sophisticated deception found in adults.[8]

Children start to express lies and engage in various coverups already by the second year! This is done at some basic level that does not have to entail false belief understanding in the strict sense of explicitly representing and theorizing about others' "tricked" mental states.

Toddlers might tell a lie because they take their desires for real (seeing enemies in wine bladders like Don Quixote) or that they might have internalized appropriate responses (reflex response to mischiefs: "No! I did not do it!") despite the fact that they actually did it.

---

[7] Woodward, A. L., Sommerville, J. A., & Guajardo, J. J. (2001). How infants make sense of intentional action. In B. F. Malle, L. J. Moses, & D. A. Baldwin (Eds.), *Intentions and intentionality* (pp. 149–169). Cambridge, MA: MIT Press.
[8] Wellman, H. (1992). *The child's theory of mind*. Cambridge, MA: MIT Press.

Researchers have systematically recorded and analyzed natural instances of lying in the home environment of two- to four-year-old children. Their conclusion: "Complex and subtle deceptive actions emerge in pragmatic contexts before a demonstrable conceptual shift in the understanding of false belief and that deceptive behavior in young pre-school children does not reduce to blind, learned strategies."[9]

In fact, the catalogue of lies and deception found in toddlers starting at two years, even if they are at basic, putatively nonstrictly representational level (i.e., without explicit false belief understanding) is stunning: from false denial ("Did you break it?" "No!"), to false blame ("I didn't do it!"), false assertion ("Not me, him!"), false excuses ("Got a belly ache"), bravado ("I am not tired"), false boasts ("I have one, too"), and feigned ignorance ("Don't know who did it").[10]

Aside from anecdotes and parental reports, experimental research at laboratories, where young children are placed in hidden-camera situations with the temptation to cheat and lie to an experimenter, documents the development of lying in three major steps. A first level of primary lies emerges starting at two to three years when children, as previously discussed, begin *deliberately* to make "factually untrue statements."[11] A second level is observed from age four when children begin to engage in deceptions that entail the understanding that others are susceptible to false beliefs. However, at this age, children are still fragile in their lies, not particularly resistant at leaking the truth or confessing that they are actually lying or cheating. Finally, at a third and final stage, children seven years and older begin to lie in ways that are analogous to adult deceptive ways. They develop to become apt and bullet-proof liars, maintaining consistency between their initial lie and follow-up statements.[12]

Like savvy criminals and defense lawyers, children by seven years become proficient at creating imaginary decoy stories and building convincing alibi. Strategically, they construct a world out of their own imagination to gain affiliation and create value for themselves, bringing the child on a collision course with morality. From this point on, children develop the human

[9] Newton, P., Reddy, V., & Bull, R. (2000). Children's everyday deception and performance in false-belief tasks. *Journal of Developmental Psychology, 18*, 297–317.
[10] Ibid.
[11] Talwar, V., & Lee, K. (2008). Social and cognitive correlates of children's lying behavior. *Child Development, 79*, 866–881.
[12] Evans, A.D. & Lee, K. (2013). Emergence of Lying in Very Young Children. *Developmental Psychology*, January, 1–6.

potential for untamed and unmatched Machiavellian intelligence, the complex strategic deception, omission of truth, deliberate concealment of reality, exaggeration, boasting, and downright lying to preserve reputation and internal consistency. All of it is an absolute necessity to navigate and survive the social world. It is also a major source of moral ambiguity.

24

Natural Roots of Moral Hypocrisy

As newborns open their eyes, glancing for the first time outside the womb, what do they experience? Research shows that they do not just experience light. From the get-go, they perceive objects and forms that detach from the ground: faces looking at them, silhouettes and objects of distinctive colors and shapes passing by. When newborns are carried around or turn their head to track and even reach for objects moving close to them, they do not confound their own action with those of moving objects. Newborns do have a proprioceptive experience of their own body as differentiated from other entities in the environment.

Numerous studies show that we are not born in William James's blooming, buzzing confusion. Rather, we are equipped with a brain, hence a mind, that perceives information and makes sense of the world with "objectivity," meaning with basic objective discrimination between self and world and also between entities in the world that exist independently of the self.

That is the basic, obligatory information processing and cognitive constraint we appear to be born with. It is a constraint evolved by the species and that we actually share with all perceiving creatures, from the chick that imprints and follows its mother like its own shadow to the just-born pups or calves latching onto their mother's tits. These newly born, like us, do not confound what is their object of attachment, and what is not. They have the innate propensity to discriminate and categorize. This is how the mind of all animals is constrained to work, and if we want to understand what's behind any of our cognitive outputs and ways we represent the world, including the ways of our adult moral hypocrisy and acrobatics, we do have to anchor this question first and foremost in this basic natural propensity expressed from birth and constituting the essence of how we think: in black and white. This is a natural process that is our obligatory lens through which we are forced to see and construe the world in our mind, including what's right and what's wrong.

Probably the most telling and robust findings of these past 50 years in the domain of infancy research pertain to newborns phonemic discrimination,

Moral Acrobatics. Philippe Rochat, Oxford University Press (2021). © Oxford University Press.
DOI: 10.1093/oso/9780190057657.003.0024

the way they perceive and discriminate speech sounds such as "pa" and "ba." With headphones on and using sucking as a response, newborns are shown to quickly differentiate the two categories of sound when presented in a continuous stream that progressively and with minute steps transforms acoustically the speech sound from "pa" to "ba". Newborns demonstrate that they do not simply perceive the continuous stream of syllables changing over time in a continuous fashion. They actually perceive "pa" up to a breaking point, a precise threshold where they detect a change and, abruptly, start to perceive "ba."

The abrupt transition from perceiving "pa" to "ba" in the continuous and monotonous stream of progressive changes in the auditory stimulus demonstrates that from birth infants are perceiving categorically, equipped to automatically discriminate and parse things into groups, not perceiving a continuous flux of stimuli streamed through their senses.[1] As a matter of fact, research shows that chinchillas presented with a continuous stream of "da" morphing into "ta" do the same. At a breaking point in the stream, they detect a categorical change.[2]

Categorical perception is indeed a very basic mental process that is pervasive in nature and that we share with all animals, from chicks to rodents. It is expressed in infants from the get-go, even in the context of their immature visual acuity. Newborns are born objective and categorical perceivers not only in the auditory domain of speech perception, but also in relation to color and face discrimination, for example.

Numerous studies show that from birth infants do perceive colors categorically, born attracted to the canonical, hence categorical configuration of face-like displays (eyes, nose and mouth organized in a Y shape). By nine months, they already show an "other race effect." Like us adults, they have significantly more difficulties in discriminating faces that are not of their own familiar ethnic group. Likewise, in relation to speech sounds, infants rapidly become discriminant of speech contrasts that are relevant to their own language, paradoxically becoming less discriminant of all other speech contrasts they are capable of perceiving from the get-go as newborns.

This phenomenon is part of what is known as *perceptual narrowing*, a categorical trimming and clustering of perceptual information, robustly

[1] Eimas, P. D., Siqueland, E. R., Jusczyk, P., & Vigorito, J. (1971). Speech perception in infants. *Science, 171*(3968), 303–306.
[2] Kuhl, P. K., & Miller, J. D. (1975). Speech perception by the chinchilla: Voiced-voiceless distinction in alveolar plosive consonants. *Science, ns 190*(4209), 69–72.

documented across perceptual domains in species from birds learning the dialect song of their species, to all mammals categorically parsing their perceptual world between what falls within the familiar as opposed to the unfamiliar: mother versus stranger, predators versus peers, in-group versus out-group members. That is the bottom-line, basic process by which minds process information from the bottom up. The ultimate function of such processes is eventually to generate predictions necessary for the survival of the individual. Again, in the broadest sense, the main function of any brain is to predict what's going to happen next.

In support of this process and according to a blueprint of basic anatomical structures developing very rapidly within the first weeks of gestation, brains are organized in neural networks that are pruned and carved as a function of experience.

The mindboggling, obligatory, and predetermined biological momentum forging the human brain machinery, essentially in support of that process, is most evident when considering that it takes only 4 weeks from conception (from the moment sperm and egg meet) for the stem structure of the brain (the neural tube) to be formed from layers of cells on the embryonic disc.[3] Only *one* extra week is needed for the basic five-part structure of the brain to be anatomically differentiated and clearly visible (i.e., telencephalon and diencephalon of the forebrain, midbrain, hindbrain, and the spinal cord). By 11 weeks of gestation (less than three months after conception!), medulla, cerebellum, inferior and superior colliculus, and both cerebral hemispheres covering the diencephalon are also clearly visible.[4]

So if we share with most animals the propensity to perceptually discriminate via a basic process of categorization, from the bottom up, the question is, What is special about human categorization, and at what point did humans diverge in their development to become the uniquely self-conscious and moral creatures we are, with all of our incomparable conscience dilemmas and moral acrobatics?

The human ontogenetic (developmental) unique bifurcation compared to other animal ontogenies is the emergence of *make beliefs*. It is when, from around two years of age, children start seamlessly to switch from discriminating and categorizing, as well as recombining categories in the here and

---

[3] Hepper, P. G. (2002). Prenatal development. In A. Slater & M. Lewis, (Eds.), *Introduction to infant development* (pp. 47–63). New York, NY: Oxford University Press.
[4] Carlson, B. M. (1994). *Human embryology and developmental biology*. St Louis, MO: Mosby.

now of perception and action, to start doing the same thing but in the realm of realities that exist only in their heads, the internal products of their own imagination. In other words, it is when the infinitely powerful and generative work of human imagination takes over. From this point on and at an exponential rate, the engagement of the basic process of discrimination and categorization operates on "decoupled" realities. This is what primarily set us apart in Nature, from a general psychological and cognitive perspective.

We are indeed part of a symbolic and referential species capable of incomparable recursive inferences (I think that she thinks that I think that he thinks). It is a given that we are incomparable at that, and it starts full blown from the middle of the second year with the vocabulary explosion, but also when toddlers start synchronously to dwell in pretend play, engaging in the simulation of reality rather than just perceiving and acting on it. They bring bananas to an ear pretending they talk on a phone, they move pieces of soap in the air making airplane noises, and they start to trick and lie, deliberately producing false truth to gain control over the attention of others and avoid their reprimands. From two years on, children open up a novel and comparatively unique horizon of development of endless possibilities, the generation of endless possible worlds, including multiple interpersonal spheres and zones of comfort as discussed in preceding chapters. This is where moral hypocrisy finds its natural roots, including all forms of essentialism discussed earlier.

From the second year, children start to act out increasingly in imagination, becoming symbolic in their play, exponentially metaphorical and referential in their communication. This is a major step toward becoming part of the decoupling prone species we are. We can hold two views on things: what they are and what we want them to be. Other species, in comparison, as sophisticated as they actually are, do not manage to decouple and meta-represent (represent representations) the same way we do. They don't have the complex language all children acquire by their second year; they do not reach the levels of our cooperation nor the human potential for perversion and evil. Yet, in the end, all this development and evolution are just different expressions of needs and concerns we share with all other social species: affiliation, closeness, safety, warmth, food, comfort. They all deal fundamentally with issues of survival and uncertainties, the necessity of controlling our physical and social environment.

In humans, it all boils down to the basic need to affiliate, the struggle for recognition, and the self-conscious concern for reputation. What is different compared to other species is the symbolic spin-off of such needs and concerns. Such spin-off is the product of a bootstrapping process by which decoupled "parallel" worlds are imagined, construed in our heads as constitutive of essential characteristics that, in fact, do not exist for real. They are simple short-cut inferences from surface characteristics leading to fundamental attribution errors—for example, that the poor are poor because they are essentially lazy. In this categorical process, imagined essential characteristics feed onto themselves *ad libitum*, bringing the dual centrifugal (exclusion) and centripetal (inclusion) processes that underlie categorization to unmatched levels of prejudice and moral judgment.

Such symbolic bootstrapping processes are the natural sources of our moral blind spots, short cuts, prejudices, and other stereotypes discussed in previous chapters. It is also the source of our spherical alliances as social categories, each loaded with different affective and emotional values that we typically juggle with, from context to context, each calling for different roles, different fronts, and codes of conduct. From family to friends and short-term acquaintances, team members, parishioners, foreigners and citizens to business partners, wife, husband, lovers, or co-workers. Each categorical sphere of alliance calls for different morals that when brought together is source of marked contradictions: loving father in one sphere, terrorist or perverted killer in another. Vegetarian animal lover on one hand, and mastermind of the Holocaust on the other.

The natural roots of moral hypocrisy and other blatant moral inconsistencies are to be found not only in the categorical discrimination process embedded in our brains, a process that—from the outset—we share with all other mindful animals. These roots are also and more specifically to be found in the bootstrapping and recursive inference mechanisms that feed onto themselves. These mechanisms bring children by the second year to the incomparable symbolic and "decoupled" levels of our own self-conscious imagination. It is this imagination that parses the world in essential clusters as a function of particular spherical alliances each defining particular moral contexts. These contexts call for character roles that are often deeply irreconcilable, only manageable for those endowed with a compartmentalized mind. This compartmentalization is at the origins of our moral acrobatics and the human propensity to think about the world in black and white.

25

What About Culture and Development?

As a last chapter of this section on the developmental origins of moral acrobatics, it is important to address the question of culture, in particular
whether compartmentalized ethical views, moral double standards, and
thinking in black and white are particularly prevalent and fostered in children of some cultures and less in others. One could easily argue that what
has been discussed in this book is mainly relevant to Western neo-liberal and
individualistic cultural contexts, and that moral acrobatics would have much
less relevance, for example, for those individuals growing up into more rural,
traditional, face-to-face, collectivistic, and intimate cultures that still prevail
in today's global world. The question is the following: Would some cultures
foster more self-unity in children, who grow up as adults who are less prone
to double standards and thinking the world in black and white?

Cross-cultural and developmental evidence suggests that having compartmentalized moral compasses and etiquettes is not unique to the WEIRD[1]
developmental niche. But why? One basic reason is that at the core of any
moral system, regardless of culture, there is the tension between self-interest
and the common interest of the group in which the individual lives to cooperate and share with others. With certainly marked differences in expression, what cuts across any culture is the basic normative moral fact that
common interest—what contributes to the group as opposed to the selfish
interest of the individual—is elevated at a positive value. This can be considered as the norm in any society, the ideal overarching rule of any normative
moral system. Across cultures, self-serving interests tends to be considered
as wrong or bad, negatively evaluated, and reprehensible. Arguably, it is the
basic ethic law naturally sanctioning cooperation and group cohesion across
human societies.

---

[1] Acronym for White, educated, industrial, rich, and democratic, the characteristics of the vast
majority of participants sampled and tested in current cognitive science research; see Heinrich, J.,
Heine, S. J., & Nrenzayan, A. (2010). The weirdest people in the world? *Behavioral and Brain Science*,
33(2–3), 61–83.

Moral Acrobatics. Philippe Rochat, Oxford University Press (2021). © Oxford University Press.
DOI: 10.1093/oso/9780190057657.003.0025

All children are exposed to this human norm, even if this norm is some-times expressed in paradoxical individualistic ways as in the "potlatch" of Native Americans of northwestern tribes studied by pioneer anthropolo-gist Franz Boas and described by Marcel Mauss. In potlatch rituals, the in-dividual of a group can destroy goods, instead of sharing them with others. It is an ostentatious act of displaying disinterest and the public contempt of receiving back from others. Yet this individualistic expression is profoundly paradoxical as it is a staged expression of absolute giving on the part of the individual with presumably no possible barter or return from others: the ex-pression of ultimate obliteration of selfish interests. Mauss writes in his sem-inal book *The Gift*[2]:

> In some instances, the point is not even of giving and giving back, but to destroy so to give the impression to the recipient that you are not even in-terested in getting something back. Houses and thousands of blankets are burned down, the most expensive copper pieces are destroyed, all that in order to crush, to flatten his rival.

The same paradox exists in Melanesian "Big Man" cultures where indi-viduals rise in social rank by individually and selfishly assembling vast wealth, often over long periods of time and with much stressful efforts, in the sole goal to throw a one-time lavish party and celebration for the group. Individuals give out in one-shot goods systematically and selfishly accumu-lated over months or even years.[3]

As a normative rule and across cultures, freeloaders tend to be scolded, and self-sacrificing individuals to the common good, decorated and rewarded. Even if sometime this rule is expressed in paradoxical ways and in multiple forms, it is a universal social law. It guides all human groups, albeit differently interpreted by individuals depending on their culture.[4] In the social realm, this law is like gravity-guiding objects in the physical world. Analogous to cultural variations, the law of gravity remains essentially the same but wears

---

[2] Mauss. (1952/1967). *The gift: Forms and functions of exchange in archaic societies*. New York, NY: Norton, pp. 201–202.

[3] See, for example, the remarkable case ethnography in Strathern, A. (1971). *The rope of Moka: Big-men and ceremonial exchange in Mount Hagen, New Guinea*. Cambridge, England: Cambridge University Press.

[4] Henrich, J., Boyd, R., Bowles, S., Camerer, C. F., Fehr, E., Gintis, H., . . . Tracer, D. (2005). "Economic man" in cross-cultural perspective: Behavioral experiments in 15 small-scale societies. *Behavioral and Brain Sciences, 28*(6), 795–815; discussion 815–855.

different clothes depending on whether it is in an aquatic or aerial environment, at high altitude or deep in the ocean. The same force is at play but with different expressions depending on circumstances.

Attached to this fundamental and universal ethics law is the subjective sense of *fairness*, what individuals consider their right share of the resources and what they are entitled to. Fairness pertains to the strong, often elusive sense we have of who deserves what and why in relation to others. As elusive as it might be, this sense is manifest remarkably early in development. And this is true regardless of vastly different social and cultural environments.

Variations do exist in the magnitude and expression of equity in early development depending on the child's sociocultural circumstances, whether, for example, the child grows up in a small-scale, face-to-face rural society or in a large, modern, urban environment. However, our own research with children from around the world—from communist China and rural Peru to middle-class America, Samoa, and street children of Brazil—demonstrates that between three and five years of age, children systematically develop a strong sense of equity in sharing.[5]

When you ask children to decide how to share a small, either even or odd number of valuable items like coins or candies, by three years, all tend to give significantly more to themselves. Such self-maximizing distribution is markedly and universally reduced by five years. The only cross-cultural difference we found in this development is that three-year-olds growing up in small-scale, traditional face-to-face communities, like the children we tested in Peru or Samoa, tended to be less selfish to start with, thus demonstrating a less steep development toward equity by five years. But by this age, children were comparable in the tendency toward equal sharing, somehow overcoming their starting state tendency toward selfishness and self-maximizing. From self-interest, children become rapidly guided by concerns that implicitly validate the common good.

What lead children between three and five years toward more equity remains a complex and open question with no simple answers. It is indeed hard to teach a child to become less selfish, and there is no ready-made educational recipe, despite many theories, including religious theories regarding how this should happen, from modeling generosity to scolding early signs of selfishness.

[5] Rochat, P., Dias, M. D. G., Guo, L., Broesch, T., Passos-Ferreira, C., Winning, A., & Berg, B. (2009). Fairness in distributive justice by 3- and 5-year-olds across 7 cultures. *Journal of Cross-Cultural Psychology*, 40(3), 416–442.

For comparison, and to probe the impact of children's early immersion into other concern, mindfulness philosophy, and systematic compassion practices, we tested a group of refugee Tibetan children growing up in a traditional Buddhist school in Dharamshala, Northern India.[6] We found that these children are not different from any other children in their development of justice distribution. Between three and five years, they demonstrate the very same developmental pattern, from selfish to more altruistic sharing, at the exact same pace compared to other children from seven radically different cultures. Three-year-old Tibetan children even tended to show more, not less, self-maximizing tendencies than three-year-olds from Trump country.

In yet another study,[7] we demonstrated that U.S. middle-class five-year-olds, in addition to becoming more equitable in their sharing, also became morally "principled": they are willing to sacrifice some of their acquired resources to punish an unfair or selfish other. By five years, children begin to manifest what is technically called "costly punishment," capable of sacrificing some of their own resources to punish an unfair other. We showed that when given the opportunity, five-year-olds will pay with some of their earned coins to penalize a puppet that behaved selfishly in a previous sharing bout. By five, children start to behave like an adult in the context of an ultimatum game, refusing an intrinsically advantageous offer that the participant perceives as too low, hence too selfish and inequitable. This tendency toward inequity aversion develops in the same way and at a similar pace from around five years across highly contrasted cultures.[8]

Recent studies indicate that long before children start to manifest inequity aversion and begin to act upon it via costly punishment or ethical protests like "Not fair!" they do have some sense of fairness in relation to others. Already by two years and even in infancy, children manifest the rudiments of fairness sentiment. For example, they tend to prefer interacting with someone who previously showed generosity as opposed to selfishness.[9] Thus it seems that there is something very primordial as to what make us universally and deeply

---

[6] Robbins, E., Starr, S., & Rochat, P. (2016). Fairness and Distributive Justice by 3–5 Year-Old Tibetan Children. *APA Journal of Cross-Cultural Psychology, 47*(3), 333–340.

[7] Robbins, E., & Rochat, P. (2011). Emerging signs of strong reciprocity in human ontogeny. *Frontiers in Psychology, 2*(353), 1–14.

[8] McAuliffe, K., Blake, P. R., Steinbeis, N., & Warneken, F. (2017). The developmental foundations of human fairness. *Nature Human Behavior, 1,* 0042.

[9] Hamlin, J. K., & Wynn, K. (2011). Young infants prefer prosocial to antisocial others. *Cognitive Development, 26,* 30–39.

sensitive to equity by age five. Maybe this sensitivity rests on propensities we inherit from evolution, as Paul Bloom and others have suggested.[10] The jury is out, and the possible mechanisms that would ultimately drive such development are still up for grabs.

What is important here and in relation to the topic of this book is the fact that in human ontogeny and across cultures, from five years of age, individuals have developed all the basic ingredients to face and deal with others' as well as their own moral conundrums. They step right into the main plot of the human drama that, from time immemorial, plays out in myths, oral tales, and tragic representations across all human cultures.

---

[10] Bloom, P. (2013). *Just babies: The origins of good and evil.* New York: NY: Random House.

Conclusion

Human Moral Frailty

In what is considered the first major literary theory in the history of Western ideas, Aristotle (*Poetics*, 335 BCE) proposes that the essence of tragedy as a major literary genre is the main character's *moral ambiguity*. Accordingly, the tragic hero is portrayed in a moral limbo. He writes:

> A perfect tragedy should, as we have seen, be arranged not on the simple but on the complex plan. It should, moreover, imitate actions which excite pity and fear, this being the distinctive mark of tragic imitation. It follows plainly, in the first place, that the change of fortune presented must not be the spectacle of a virtuous man brought from prosperity to adversity: for this moves neither pity nor fear; it merely shocks us. Nor, again, that of a bad man passing from adversity to prosperity: for nothing can be more alien to the spirit of Tragedy; it possesses no single tragic quality; it neither satisfies the moral sense nor calls forth pity or fear. Nor, again, should the downfall of the utter villain be exhibited. A plot of this kind would, doubtless, satisfy the moral sense, but it would inspire neither pity nor fear; for pity is aroused by unmerited misfortune, fear by the misfortune of a man like ourselves. Such an event, therefore, will be neither pitiful nor terrible. There remains, then, the character between these two extremes—that of a man who is not eminently good and just, yet whose misfortune is brought about not by vice or depravity, but by some error or frailty. (Aristotle, *Poetics,* Section 2, Part XIII)

Since the Greeks, great tragedies rest on character's moral frailty and ambiguity as the engine of misfortunes, the essential ingredient making a good tragedy within the Aristotelian system. From Oedipus Rex, Hamlet, and Dr. Faustus to Rodion Raskolnikov, all great Western tragedies do tend to have in common the representation of tragic flaws in the main character. *Tragic flaw* is actually a technical term used to describe the literary device that would define tragedy as a literary genre.

Moral Acrobatics. Philippe Rochat, Oxford University Press (2021). © Oxford University Press.
DOI: 10.1093/oso/9780190057657.001.0001

If character flaws and moral acrobatics are central pieces of major Western literary productions, notwithstanding movies, questions remain regarding their universal relevance, whether they are of the same central appeal in other oral and literate cultures from around the world. Following Aristotle, *catharsis* would be the single purification and purging mechanism of emotions behind spectators' appeal to spectacular, especially tragic contents. For Aristotle, good tragedies are those that trigger fear and pity in the audience members, somehow fortifying them emotionally through an elusive process of emotional renewal and restoration. Freud re-appropriated the concept of catharsis (literally purification or cleansing in ancient Greek) to describe the emotional renewal and restoration gained by patients reminiscing and re-enacting tragic childhood events during their psychoanalytical cure.

If catharsis remains a valid concept that carries with it the potential to account for the spectacular appeal of dramas involving heroic central characters, the question is whether moral frailty is also a universal ingredient of good dramas (following Aristotle) beyond the Western context. Do we find the same centrality of prototypical heroes' tragic flaws and existential conflicts of interest in oral myths, literary, or movie productions from around the world?

It appears that there is indeed something universal and transcultural in the moral content of human artistic propensities to represent existence with its torments and primordial moral conflicts. Although marked cultural differences exist in the way such conflicts are staged and thought of for public representations, all can be said to help audience and participants to find solace by conjuring (purifying?) fears and uncertainties that are inherent to human self-conscious mortal nature. The staging by imitation (*mimesis*) of existential realities in various rituals and other mimetic art forms is a fundamental expression of human nature in general. For millennia it has been expressed across all cultures in various forms, from religious sacrifices, ancestral Indian epic poems like the Ramayana reverberating across Asia, or the Noh theater in Japan, to classic and neo-classic tragedy in the Greek tradition. Mimesis is a trait that arguably distinguishes us from other animals,[1] and as I see it a direct spin-off of human self-consciousness, in particular the inner conflicts arising from the unsettling awareness of one's own, irremediable mortality.

---

[1] For further discussion, see Melvin Donald (1991). *Origins of the modern mind: three stages in the evolution of culture and cognition.* Cambridge (MA): Harvard University Press.

The pull toward dramatic representation of human fate and existence is a fact of human life. Above and beyond the great diversity of forms and cultural expressions of such pull, it can be understood as a universal drive to conjure shared fears and frailties, moral frailties in particular as it relates to virtue, the good as opposed to the bad. The point is that across cultures, moral frailty and associated moral acrobatics appear to be an issue at the core of much human spectacular appeal, albeit expressed in various genres, from classic tragedy in the West (Greek, Elizabethan, French, or modern novels and plays) to more ritualistic and lyrical forms in the East (ancient epic poem like the Ramayana in India that permeates all Southeast Asia over centuries, or the ancient Noh theater in Japan), but also as we will see in more primitive rituals and ceremonies among indigenous people living in remote places.

There are obviously some fundamental cross-cultural differences in the mimesis of human existential turmoil and conflicts and profound differences in aesthetic approaches to the human artful reflection on life and our place in the universe. In classic Western tragedy, and since the Greeks, the focus is on the individual tragic hero, clinging to life and its vicissitudes. This is particularly exemplified in the offshoots that are Shakespeare's Elizabethan plays, but also the French tragedies of the 17th century by Racine or Corneille, in which heroes are exposed "from the inside—as he struggles to assert himself and his values against whatever would deny them."[2] Think Romeo and Juliet.

In Eastern traditions, either in the Ramayana, the Noh theater, but also in Chinese traditional theater, heroes tend to be more subordinated to the flow of fateful events, submitted to the forces of tradition and ancestry, and less driven by internal torments that are at the core of Western tragedies à la Shakespeare.[3]

In Japan, Noh theater is a 700-year-old tradition, a classic performing art form still rigorously staged today. It continues to be a cultivated and treasured drama tradition with the particularity that the hero wears a mask. There is today a repertory of 250 plays that continue to be performed at various theaters in Japan. These plays were mainly created during a state

---

[2] Sewall, R. B., & Conversi, L. W. (2000). Tragedy, literature article. Online *Encyclopaedia britannica*.

[3] "Thus, Noh avoids directly involving the audience in the emotions implicit in the events portrayed on the stage. It gives only a slight hint of the spiritual struggle in the heart of the protagonist—a struggle that is always speedily resolved in favour of traditional teaching. In play after play the action does not take place on stage but is reenacted by the ghost of one of the participants. Thus, the events presented are tinged with memory or longing—hardly the primary emotions that surge through and invigorate Western tragedy at its best." Ibid.

of great conflicts (the warring states period or Sengoku jidai) in the 15th-century that lasted for about 150 years. They consist of legends and stories of the Muromachi Period (1336–1573) when Noh emerged. At the time, warriors governed the country and were the ruling class, allowing the performing art to develop and reflect values specifically attached to this governing cast. Aside from staging canons of elegant beauty to the audience, the content of the plays exemplifies mainly for the audience templates of good conscience around norms of military virtues for which spectators can project for themselves. Courage, dignity, fidelity, and unwavering integrity in the midst of conflicts and dangers are exemplified by the masked hero in Noh representations. Yet, the focus is not as much on the internal conflicts driving the prototypical hero of Western tragedies. It is rather the force of external and situational factors that eventually drives the individual hero toward peace and harmony with the world. The same can be said of the Indian Ramayana tale, a very widespread story-line influence all over Far Eastern cultures, Indian, but also Sikh and Buddhist ancestral traditions.

Distinct from the story-line acted out in the Noh theater, the Ramayana tale exemplifies virtues, conduct codes, and good and bad etiquettes embodied by powerful enticing characters in their fateful journey back home after a long forced and eventful separation. It is overall the storyline of Homer's *Odyssey*, which appears to be remarkably recurrent across cultures, conjuring, in my mind, the deep universal fear of social rejection and separation.[4] Ramanaya is an ancient Indian Epic poem tracing back to the 7th century BCE. It continues to inspire pictorial and theatrical representations in almost all Far East Indian and Buddhist traditions, including Thailand, Cambodia, Malaysia, Indonesia, and Bali in particular. Its narration is perpetuated to this day through various versions adapted to vast cultural and religious regions of the Far East. It narrates the odyssey of divine Prince Rama, his struggle with his father and a demon king who kidnaps his wife, until his return and final crowning. The tale of Prince Rama is a tale of virtue, patience, and courage through the ordeal of a forced 14-year exile rewarded by his final return to govern and create an ideal state.

Back to the intent of this discussion, the struggle to calibrate one's own moral compass is arguably the meta-theme of mimesis across cultures. The joy and enticement of spectacular representation of characters and life events are universal, present in all cultures from aboriginal dance ceremonies in

---

[4] See Rochat, P. (2009). *Others in Mind*. Cambridge University Press.

Papua New Guinea (see following discussion) to most rule-ridden and re-
fined theatrical traditions like Noh or Elizabethan plays. It continues to be
the case with the new wave of Netflix series. There are, however, marked
differences in the nature and psychological underpinnings of mimesis
across cultures. As we have seen, in the Western tradition, tragic characters
are put on public display to act out their inner conflicts, eaten up by moral
contradictions and inner questioning, such as to be or not to be? For Hamlet,
how to live with revengeful feelings followinghis father's death, or for
Oedipus, after realizing that he slept with his mother and killed his father?
In the Western tradition, the focus tends to be what is happening within the
individual, and less what is happening around him, namely situations and
the surrounding community. Nonetheless, I would argue, there is the same
meta-function of mimesis across these very different aesthetics or cultural
approaches to the human dilemma, it is the need to reflect upon and recali-
brate one's own moral compass—getting enticed and inspired by stories and
their protagonists that conjure fear of excessive situations and the power of
inner drives, in particular love, jealousy, shame, attachment, and its necessary counterpart, the human deep fear of separation.[5] This meta-function
is arguably what drives artistic and ceremonial traditions from around the
world. Each tradition is associated with various forms of representations
corresponding to markedly different aesthetics, hence sensibilities that are
adjusted to the group's ways of being together, in the same way that religious
ceremonies and denominations vary around the world. But all religions are
different forms of representation regarding the universal human questions
of where one comes from, where one is going once gone, and, more important, how to behave while alive. Here again, and in addition to being able to
conjure basic fears, finding solace, as well as courage, what mimesis universally offers to an audience is the opportunity to reflect upon moral conducts
and adjust one's own moral compass in the face of inescapable, hence transcultural, moral conundrums, and ambiguities. Regardless of culture, all
individuals are under the spell of greedy temptations and other parochial
tendencies that go against the larger collective good. That is a universal
reason for the existence of explicit moral values emulated in mimesis all over
the world with all its diverse aesthetics that evolved over time, across societies and historic circumstances. It is their common denominator. Culture
and related forms of mimesis are nothing more than *particular expressions*

[5] Ibid.

of the same self-conscious psychology that is specific to our species. Advanced civilizations and world religions offer various forms of mimesis in rituals (prayers, celebrations, staged reunions) and in stories consigned in sacred books (Bible, Qur'an, Talmud) for the same opportunity to confront and calibrate one's own frail moral compass, to find guidance and adjustments in our decisions and attitudes toward others, to find reprieve and repentance for self under the permanent spell of potential guilt, another uniquely human and universal curse, the product of our self-conscious psychology.

Across societies, mimesis allows individuals to confront their own moral frailty, itself a universal and the topic of this book. Rituals and epic tales of all genres are indeed deeply confrontational to an audience. It is in essence provocative, as all mimesis are meant to trigger particular feelings and emotions leading to the perennial tension between love and separation, power and grief. This seems particularly true looking at the ethnography of more traditional, isolated, and small-scale ("primitive") societies like the Inuit.

Anthropologist Jean Briggs[6] documents for example the education of young three- year-old girls growing up in an Inuit Baffin Island hunting camp on the Arctic shore. Her work shows that the child is systematically teased by adults with playful yet emotionally filled dilemma with dangerous choices, such as "Are you good?"; "Is your mother good?"; "Do you want to live with me" ... ? Following the questions, adults tend to dramatize the consequences based on the child's answer, such as "Ok, then I am going to bring you to this faraway floe and leave you out there alone." Briggs shows the pervasiveness of such dramatic tease-play with the child, the mark of what she identifies as an essential force in the social life of the Inuit. Dramatic enactment, such as tease-play, is yet another form of mimesis helping the child to conjure fears and find direction in the face of conflicts and other emotionally charged situations. Briggs argues that it is through this kind of dramatic tease-play that Inuit children learn primarily to resolve moral conundrums and conflicts.

Another more tropical example showing the universal dimension of catharsis through mimesis is the ethnography of staged ceremonies by the Kalui people living in the high plateau of Papua New Guinea, poignantly described by anthropologist Edward Shieffelin in his book, *The Sorrow of the Lonely and the Burning of the Dancers.*[7] Shieffelin shows that ceremonies among the Kalui are pretexts to stage and demonstrate reciprocity among themselves, within

---

[6] Briggs, J. L. (1999). *Inuit morality play. The emotional education of a three-year-old.* New Haven, CT: Yale University Press.
[7] Shieffelin, E. L. (1976). *The sorrow of the lonely and the burning of the dancers.* New York, NY: St Martin Press

and across villages and so-called long-houses. Gift giving and the staging of reciprocity are at the core of all cultures of the South Pacific, extensively documented since the work of pioneer anthropologists Bronislaw Malinowski on the ritual circle of exchanges (kula) in the Solomon islands. It is also, for the Kalui of Papua New Guinea, pretext to explore and conjure in catharsis the tragedy of loss and sorrow, an opportunity to express anger and revenge within the confines of pretense and play, not unlike what was offered in the mimesis of ancient Greek tragedies or at the Globe theater in Shakespeare's time. Here is how Shieffelin describes the *Gisaro* ceremony, the main "most elaborated and characteristic" ceremony among the Kalui people:

> One dancer (invited from another village and clan) sang a song that alluded to the dead son of a senior of the host clan. . . . The youth had died at a small house near a creek called Abo, and his soul was believed to have gone to the treetops in the form of a bird, . . . The senior man who was sitting with the crowd at the sidelines, brooding and withdrawn, suddenly became overcome with grief and burst into loud wails of anguish. Enraged, he jumped up, grabbed a torch from a bystander and jammed the burning end forcefully into the dancer's bare shoulder. With a tremendous noise, all the youths and young men of the host community jumped into the dancing space, stamping and yelling and brandishing axes. The dancer was momentarily lost in a frightening pandemonium of shadowy figures, torches, and showers of sparks. Showing no sign of pain, he moved slowly across the dancing space; the chorus burst into song. The senior man broke away from the crowd and ran out the back door of the house to wail on the veranda. This scene was repeated over and over from dancer to dancer during the course of the night.[8] (p. 23)

In Polynesia, another region of South Pacific, the traditional insular life of the Samoan people, first famously documented by Margaret Mead in the 1920s, reveals what I view as something deep and universal about morality, something that across cultures mimesis in its various forms tries to conjure. What is revealed in Samoan culture is an expression of how we manage to overcome inherent moral uncertainty by thinking the world in black and white. Morality here is understood in the broad sense of value attribution to self and others along the binary scale of good or bad, right or wrong, virtuous or coward, guilty or not.

[8] Ibid.

The pragmatic "situationist" way Samoan people appear to resolve inherent contradictions, attached to the attribution of absolute values to self and others, is to judge them in relation to context and external situations, not in reference to invariant, context-independent properties that would be inherent to the individual or group of individuals. If Samoans are "essentialist" and absolutist in their thinking, eventually thinking in black and white like any other human beings, their essentialism and absolutist tendencies is context dependent, which might sound deeply contradictory to a Western, Cartesian, or Kantian ear.

As emphasized by the detailed ethnography of Samoa by cultural anthropologist Bradd Shore, an expert of Samoan ways of living and thinking, the Samoan language does not provide terms qualifying inner, independent properties to the self and other, such as autonomous inner mental states. In Samoan language, one talks about self and others primarily in relation to external situations, in sharp contrast to the Western Cartesian world view that tends to attribute mental states independently of context. Genuine situationists or contextualists in their moral judgments, Samoans tend to focus primarily on the particular relations individuals have with a particular situation in the environment. Situations vary as per their judgments, which often appear contradictory to foreigners (White, or *palagi* in the Samoan language). Here is what Bradd Shore notes in his seminal 1982 book, *Sala'ilua: A Samoan Mystery*:

> The sense of contradiction is . . . felt by any European new to Samoa. Samoans appear, on one hand, rigidly absolutistic in their loyalties and their judgments. On the other hand, an observer eventually gets the feeling that no judgment is absolute, and that no particular loyalty is absolute. This paradox disappears, however, once we recognize that any particular judgment is implicitly grounded in a context, and that consistency to context but not necessarily between contexts is the implicit logical basis of a Samoan moral system. . . . Samoan judgments are thus to be understood as absolute in relation to their context, but relativistic from an "objective" perspective outside any particular context. The absence of this objective perspective in Samoan thought is a fundamental fact of moral discourse in that society.[9]

---

[9] Shore, B. (1982). *Sala'ilua: A Samoan mystery.* New York, NY: Columbia University Press, pp. 191–192.

Samoans resolve the conundrum of moral decision making in a pragmatic, compartmentalized way of producing absolute moral judgments referenced to specific contexts and situations.

Coming back to the question driving this concluding chapter, namely, whether the topic of this book has universal relevance, it is important to consider this question in light of the bottom-line fact that explicit moral norms and moral values are a universal property of any human group. This property emerges from the assembly, cooperation, and reciprocal exchanges among uniquely self-conscious creatures that are endowed, among other things (i.e., symbolism and mimesis), with a unique capacity for guilt and shame. The bottom-line fact is that no human societies exist without some normative moral system, from hunter-gatherers to large civilizations. Standards and norms are indeed a unique human sociological trait, expressed in mimesis as we have seen, from ancestral times across all cultures. Now, if moral systems are universal, does it finally also apply to moral hypocrisy?

One way to address this question is to ask what might be universally amoral? As sociologist Pierre Bourdieu states in his book on practical reasons, a good starting point to reflect upon morality is to reflect upon

> the universally attested existence of second degree, meta-narrative or meta-practical strategies by which social agents aim at producing appearances of conformity to a universal rule, despite the fact that their practice is in contradiction with the rule or that it does not abide to the principle of pure obedience to the rule.[10] (p. 233)

In many ways, as suggested by Bourdieu, the best way to capture a group's rule is to look at how in practice it is bent or ignored by group members. Bourdieu mentions the Kabyle saying, "Each rule has its exit door," or "Taboos (forbidden rules) are made to be violated," as stated by pioneer anthropologist Marcel Mauss. If the bending of consensual group rules is universal, as, for example, the universal appeal to minimizing imposed taxes and to maximize benefits via cheating or the bending of the rule, it is also necessarily an expression of the acknowledgment of such a rule. By transgressing and while doing so deliberately, one recognizes the existence of what is transgressed. It does not cancel the existence of the rule, but rather ascertains it. When any society judges its transgressors, it is implicitly recognized that

---

[10] Translation from French by the author, p. 233.

the transgressor is aware of the rule that has been transgressed, a transgression that is in violation of a collective consensus. However, in any society, the recognition of such awareness in the transgressor depends on its place or status within the society. The moral hypocrisy of a high-ranking chief or politician is typically considered a greater transgression compared to the moral hypocrisy of a low-ranking commoner. Across cultures, chiefs are more accountable of their transgressions of moral rectitude as they are *the rulers*: the symbolic impersonation of the rule and its enforcement, as Bourdieu would probably say. Political scandals come from the top and the powerful, less from the bottom of any society. Think of those priests accused of pedophilia and their superiors covering it up. Which transgression is more scandalous?

Moral hypocrisy is everywhere but judged relative to rank, often repressed in inverse proportion. White-collar and other high-ranking criminals typically end up purging time in white-collar prisons or assigned to a residence (consider Manafort or Mubarak), unlike petty criminals from the slums who typically end up in overcrowded and dangerous penitentiaries (think of Brazil favelas and Brazilian prisons, the incarceration of former President Lula for corruption). The fact that everywhere justice is relative to rank is an endemic and universal moral hypocrisy. In many ways, we all are rather unequal in the face of the law. The fact that justice generally depends on rank is yet evidence of another moral conundrum and source of universal moral hypocrisy that we as moral acrobats have to deal with.

In relation to rank and justice, all individuals across human societies live in various spherical alliances, with compartmentalized moral ecosystems that sometimes can permeate and collapse (see Chapter 11 of this book). Across these interpersonal spheres, individuals tend to have different ranks and, hence, represent different symbolic impersonation of the rule governing a particular sphere: father in the family sphere; chief, commoner, or simple citizen in the political sphere; boss or employee in the work sphere. If that is a universal reality, then individuals' relation to the rule in place and their relative impersonation of that rule must change from sphere to sphere, the universal source of moral acrobatics for all individuals living in society, and this, regardless of culture.

The constant switching of relation to the rule across spherical alliances, and the necessary moral acrobatics, also entails a switching of self-presentation and moral attitude, a different impersonation of the governing rule: from dominant figure in one to lower ranking position, from various distances to the rule, from major impersonation of authority in the family sphere to subordinate in another. Often the culture scaffolds individuals in their moral acrobatics as they transit from spherical alliances to spherical alliances in their daily transactions. In Samoa, for example, the language accommodates two forms of communication, an intimate common form (intimate style *k-pronunciation* language) and a formal form (formal style *t-pronunciation* language) used alternatively in either polite or informal contexts, in other words the varying contexts of one's own spherical alliances. To a novice's ear, these two forms of exchanges sound radically different, and yet, Samoans are capable of switching from one to the other in a single conversation. It is much more than the French or German intimate versus more formal pronouns (*tu* vs. *vous; du* vs. *sie*) that typically are used systematically in one form or the other, unless signifying "interpersonal ice breaking" (switching from *sie* to *du*) or eventually "interpersonal chilling" (switching from *tu* to *vous*).

The existence of a dual phonological system, what Bradd Shore describes in his ethnography of Samoan language as large "context-bound vocabulary levels," is not unique to this culture, but is found across Far Eastern cultures, in Korean, Japanese, Javanese, Tongan, and Futunan languages in particular, all showing "a relatively elaborate division within its lexicon between common or ordinary and polite vocabulary."[11] But this palette of lexicons offered to language users as they journey across spherical alliances is not different from slang vs. proper language that exist in all cultures, used alternatively by individuals to impersonate various distance to the rule.

The forced journey across spherical alliances that universally is a foundational aspect of human sociality favors a categorical thought process of the world in black or white. This universal social journey constrains individuals, depending on their rank, constantly to switch and gauge their distance, hence following Bourdieu, their impersonation of the rule that applies within a particular spherical alliance (close family, extended family, workplace, feud with enemies, intimate couple relationship, political party, team, etc.). The transition between social contexts is typically abrupt, requiring a sudden switch of attitudes and moral hats, sudden changes of rule impersonation, from father scolding his child to answering the call of a reprimanding boss.

Overall, psychologically, such acrobatics foster sharp contrasts in thinking the world in terms of good *or* bad, right *or* wrong, just *or* unjust, individuals having to shift abruptly from different impersonation of the rule, from very

---

[11] Bourdieu, P. (1994). *La Raison Pratique. Sur la théorie de l'action.* (Practical Reason. On the theory of action). Paris: Seuil.

close impersonation (authoritarian father, dominant lover), to very distant (employee fired by his boss, individual incarcerated or repudiated from the village by its chiefs). Powerful and high ranking in one moment, submissive and low ranking in the next: multiple power hats and rule impersonations for one person.

Moral acrobatics is indeed a cross-cultural universal that fosters constant sharp shifts in moral compass depending on situation and rank within that momentous situation and how much one individual impersonates the rule recognized by others within a particular spherical alliance.

Such shifts in moral compass are part of human moral nature, a nature that has dual and conflictual battles at its core, the battle between the common good and their own welfare that varies across spherical alliances. It is the main source of the moral frailty which is, following Aristotle, the defining core of the human tragedy that continues to motivate mimesis and other spectacular public representations in all cultures.

Postscript

Moral Acrobatics and Human Violence

We cannot deal with the issue of human moral acrobatics without also
acknowledging the backdrop of the unique human propensity toward violence, from heroic self-sacrifice toward the in-group to gratuitous sadistic abuses toward the out-group. If violence pervades nature, we as a
self-conscious and symbolic species brought it to unmatched levels. Across
species, mating entails fights and often bloody violence, but not the kind of
systematic warfare humans have seemingly always dwelled in. Archeological
finds point to human-on-human massacres that well antecede recorded history. There are prehistorical traces of large-scale invasions, conquests, and
other collective massacres. It is the backdrop foundation of all great myths,
each strikingly devoid of any humor,[1] from Homer's *Odysseus* to the collected stories compiled in sacred books like the Qur'an or both Old and New
Testaments in the Bible.

Some historians and philosophers link the human bloody history of conquest wars, kin, and other massacres to unmistakable pleasures, the reliefs
(catharsis?) from envy and jealousy, the anguish reduction derived from violence and ritualistic sacrifices, all boiling down to the causing of pain and the
elimination of scapegoat others.[2] What is the sometime link to an "art" (i.e.,
the art of warfare) seems to represent a deep need to assert ourselves, the cultivation of incomparable friendship through hardship, the opportunity for
individuals to stage heroic acts of courage and altruism boosting our reputation and more often than not feeding our self-delusion. War is an opportunity to transcend one's own self-aware mundane existence, creating values
for self and those we identify with. This is what is at the core of Cervantes's

---

[1] I challenge anybody to find any jokes or intended puns in the bible, which is interestingly symp-
tomatic and too often overlooked by religious critics.
[2] See the irresistible mimetic aspect of violence and scapegoating found in primeval religions
discussed in René Girard's classic book: Girard, R. (1977). *Violence and the sacred*. Baltimore,
MD: Johns Hopkins University Press, 1977.

Moral Acrobatics. Philippe Rochat, Oxford University Press (2021). © Oxford University Press.
DOI: 10.1093/oso/9780190057657.001.0001

great character of Don Quixote who desperately seeks heroism and an assertion of chivalry and who ends up fighting an army of windmills.

Proof of such a process is the endemic depression afflicting many young
veterans returning home from the front, who, among other traumas, suffer
from drastic changes in life intensity. They abruptly shift in an existential
transition from the highs of brotherhood solidarity and the display of heroic courage in the scary yet exciting life on the frontline, to the dull lows of
reunited domesticity and its much more comfortable but predictable life on
the home front. This happens to be the central theme of most war narratives
and movies, particularly in recent bestsellers like *War* by Sebastian Junger[3]
or Hollywood productions like the 2008 *Hurt Locker* movie directed by
Kathryn Bigelow. Tales of war and aggression are indeed popular because
we live vicariously the scary acts of organized violence, a backdrop for the
revelation of heroic and cowardly characters, the pleasure of winning over
enemies and the passive experience of *Shadenfreude*, the pleasure we derive
from the misfortune of others. *Shadenfreude* is, in great part, what makes us
go to see movies or read novels. It is the pleasurable emotions we seek as we
project ourselves into fictive suffering characters on a screen or in novels.
This is undeniably unique to our species, in the same way that is unique for us
to engage since time immemorial in the nonfictional art of war among ourselves. The question is how to account for such human propensity, aside from
the human inclination toward cooperation, empathy, and all other more positive traits, the main focus of current debates on human nature in our "age of
empathy"? How to account for our darker side? Could it be a necessary complement in sharp contrast to our brighter side?

At the core of the destructive human propensity there is fear, in particular
a generalized fear of being dispossessed not only of things we get affectively
attached to and want to protect—territory, offspring, and mating partners, as
in the case for any other species—but also of abstract and essential privileges
such as property, national identity, honor, or long-term social debts that are
uniquely human concerns and construal. The human fear of dispossession
derives from our poisoned gift from nature, which is self-consciousness.
Bluntly put, I would argue that such human fear derives from the awareness
of our own mortality. It is fed by our awareness of impending separation
from others, the inescapable eventual vanishing of the embodied self, hence
also of others into oblivion. If not into oblivion, as religious faithful would

[3] Junger, S. (2010). *War*. New York, NY: Twelve.

argue, at least it is the awareness of our own vanishing from this life and all its attachments, which in the end amounts to the same thing.

Self-consciousness makes us particularly fearful and, hence, defensive, aggressive, and, in the end, uniquely dangerous to our kin. But paradoxically, I would argue that the human particularly exacerbated evil side of us is nothing but a perversion of our primal innate *goodness*. The latter is also particularly exacerbated in our species. Why so? I think it is linked to the fact that we are equipped to nurture our progenies who stay immature and dependent over years. Indeed, compared to all other ontogenies, humans have an extended period of immaturity, close to 10 years at minimum after birth, in which the child depends almost totally on the care of others who are endowed with parenting and protective instincts to sustain care for their young over such an extended period. But what about the human extreme potential for systematic violence? Could human unmatched malice be a perversion of primal goodness?

It might be the case, because we are a symbolic species, capable of decoupling our representations and the work of our imaginations. Linked to the ability to dwell in the generation of made-up beliefs and to engage in recursive inferences, it is also our unique propensity to engage in perverted acts, literally "the alteration of something from its original course, meaning, or state to a distortion or corruption of what was first intended," the dictionary definition of *perversion*.[4] As a symbolic species, it appears that we have evolved the potential to corrupt our primal intentions that are in essence good and nurturing for the survival of our progenies.

In short, a major source of human evil might be the perversion of a primal goodness evolved for the sake of our progenies and, hence, for the good of our species in its perpetuation. This said, it does not explain why, as a species, we would be so inclined to pervert what is good. Could it be driven by the cultivation of unique sadistic pleasures? Is it also possibly a drive to prevent and conjure the basic fear of being dispossessed of what we experience as entitlements? Or could it be, as I think it probably is, a combination of both?

In his book, *On the Genealogy of Morality*, Nietzsche makes the argument that there is an undeniable human taste for cruelty. This is plainly demonstrated in the justice done via bloody penal sanctions. As disturbing as it might make us feel, lust is often a close companion of our own malice and all the ills we inflict or dream to inflict onto others.

---

[4] lexico.com (Oxford Dictionary).

In relation to the human proclivity toward revenge and retaliation, Nietzsche remarks: How can one think that suffering inflicted to others can be the compensation for a debt if there was not a genuine pleasure at inflicting pain? "To make someone suffer is pleasure in its highest form, and to the degree that the injured party received an extraordinary counter-pleasure in exchange for the injury and distress caused by the injury: to make someone suffer,— a true feast."[5]

French philosopher Michel Foucault documents the historical changes in the European penal system around the revolutionary times of the 18th-century *Enlightenment*. Justice went from being expedited via the practice of public tortures and executions to set examples, to long-term prison confinement under high surveillance, forced labor, and tentative programs to re-educate criminals within penitentiary walls or even sent to designated far away colonies like Australia for Great Britain or Guyana for France. Foucault starts his famous essay with the gruesome example of prerevolution (i.e., 1757) public execution for regicide of Robert-François Damiens.

Damiens was a domestic servant who tried to kill Louis the XV of France. His execution raised much controversy and Damien ended up being the last French criminal to be executed by "drawing and quartering." This left a place for new judicial technologies for execution like beheading by the specially designed guillotine at the time of the French Revolution.

Starting his essay, Foucault writes:

> On 2 March 1757 Damiens the regicide was condemned "to make the amende honorable before the main door of the Church of Paris," where he was to be "taken and conveyed in a cart, wearing nothing but a shirt, holding a torch of burning wax weighing two pounds"; then, "in the said cart, to the Place de Grève, where, on a scaffold that will be erected there, the flesh will be torn from his breasts, arms, thighs and calves with red-hot pincers, his right hand, holding the knife with which he committed the said parricide, burnt with sulphur, and, on those places where the flesh will be torn away, poured molten lead, boiling oil, burning resin, wax and sulphur melted together and then his body drawn and quartered by four horses and his limbs and body consumed by fire, reduced to ashes and his ashes thrown to the winds."

[5] Nietzsche, F. (2006). *On the genealogy of morality* (K. Ansell-Pearson, Ed., C. Diethe, Trans.). Cambridge, England: Cambridge University Press; second essay on "guilt, bad conscience, and related matters," sixth paragraph.

Here is what Parisians were actually offered to see following the meticulous report published by the *Amsterdam Gazette* of April 1757. . . . "Finally, he was quartered. This last operation was very long, because the horses used were not accustomed to drawing; consequently, instead of four, six were needed; and when that did not suffice, they were forced, in order to cut off the wretch's thighs, to sever the sinews and hack at the joints. . . . The sulphur was lit, but the flame was so poor that only the top skin of the hand was burnt, and that only slightly. Then the executioner, his sleeves rolled up, took the steel pincers, which had been especially made for the occasion, and which were about a foot and a half long, and pulled first at the calf of the right leg, then at the thigh, and from there at the two fleshy parts of the right arm; then at the breasts. . . . After these tearings with the pincers, Damiens, who cried out profusely, though without swearing, raised his head and looked at himself; the same executioner dipped an iron spoon in the pot containing the boiling potion, which he poured liberally over each wound. Then the ropes that were to be harnessed to the horses were attached with cords to the patient's body; the horses were then harnessed and placed alongside the arms and legs, one at each limb. . . . The horses tugged hard, each pulling straight on a limb, each horse held by an executioner. After a quarter of an hour, the same ceremony was repeated and finally, after several attempts, the direction of the horses had to be changed, thus: those at the arms were made to pull towards the head, those at the thighs towards the arms, which broke the arms at the joints. This was repeated several times without success. He raised his head and looked at himself. Two more horses had to be added to those harnessed to the thighs, which made six horses in all. Without success.[6]

This report is gruesome, but not exceptional in how humans seek revenge and social justice, getting apparent pleasure or relief from it. Torture and genocide have not disappeared, despite all good public deeds to control these violent human streaks, starting with the chart of human rights written, paradoxically, by the same French revolutionaries prone to behead, not only counterrevolutionaries resisting their enlightened ideas, but also

---

[6] Foucault, M. (1975). *Discipline and punish: The birth of the prison.* New York, NY: Random House, p. 3.

systematically to massacre thousands of innocent children, sick adults, and the elderly.[7]

Freud (b. 1856–d. 1939), father of psychoanalysis and on the footsteps of philosopher Friedrich Nietzsche (b. 1844–d. 1900), recognizes that being human means to dwell on uncanny pleasures. Resonating Nietzsche's bold views on the genealogy of human morality, Freud acknowledges our inclination to derive pleasure from killing and afflicting pain on others.

In his late book of 1930 *Civilization and Its Discontents* where he reflects on the moral nature of Man, Freud writes, "There would be no reason, nor any necessity to forbid murder if Man did not aspire to it. The passion for murder is primordial and morality is a historical secondary construction." In another passage Freud famously insists on the dreadful human exception in Nature:

> Men are not gentle creatures, who want to be loved, who at the most can defend themselves if they are attacked; they are, on the contrary, creatures among whose instinctual endowments is to be reckoned a powerful share of aggressiveness. As a result, their neighbor is for them not only a potential helper or sexual object, but also someone who tempts them to satisfy their aggressiveness on him, to exploit his capacity for work without compensation, to use him sexually without his consent, to seize his possessions, to humiliate him, to cause him pain, to torture and to kill him. *Homo homini lupus* (Man is wolf to Man). Who in the face of all his experience of life and of history, will have the courage to dispute this assertion?

Researchers mock this view for two reasons. First, by pointing out that Freud's statement derides canines' capacity for prosocial and cooperative behavior, which is now taken by canine specialists as inaccurate.[8] And, second, because Freud's view tends to deride what might be the better angel of our nature, our fundamentally good and prosocial proclivities, in line for example with the Dalai Lama's well-intended push toward secular ethics.[9] We

---

[7] Infamous example of such is, circa 1793 so-called Vendée's wars during the Terror era of the French revolution, the systematic drowning by republican revolutionaries of thousands (not hundreds, thousands) of elderlies and sick adults as well as children embarked on flat bottom barges and sunk by night in the middle of the Loire river by the city of Nantes.

[8] de Waal, Frans (2006). *Primates and Philosophers: How Morality Evolved*. Princeton, NJ: Princeton University Press, p. 3.

[9] de Waal, F. (2006). *Primates and philosophers: How morality evolved*. Princeton, NJ: Princeton University Press, p. 3.; HH The Dalai Lama. (2011). *Beyond religion: Ethics for a whole world*. New York, NY: Houghton Mifflin.

have to acknowledge, however, that this line of criticisms is difficult to reconcile with the human creativity in the art of war, and in particular with the universal sense of ease and relief we experience when justice is done. However,
as previously suggested, the evil side of humans might just be a perversion
of a good, a perversion driven by self-consciousness and its necessary companion, which is the deep fear of vanishing and being dispossessed.

Above all, we protect ourselves and our privileges, preserve our reputation
as insurance of future comfort for self but also for those we care for and identify with. First and foremost, let us not lose track of the fact that we generate
values for ourselves and those we identify with. We protect our own comfort and privileges, the comfort of our family and friends, our paycheck, the
projects and ambitions we live by.

In the end, we all run our own little living enterprise, driven primarily to
yield values for self and selected others: associates, family kin, supporters,
co-workers, partners, clients, chosen friends, admirers, future conquests,
political allies. In this process, we necessarily create privileges that promote
inequality and give room for decoupled double standards. Ethical rules are
switched depending on the circle and the interest of our living enterprise,
the source of our privileges. That is fundamentally what we all so desperately try to keep afloat with feelings of uncertainty and the fearful threat
that it all could sink at any time, be it in a family feud, job loss, rejection,
being rebuffed, betrayed, falling sick, becoming suddenly unemployed, or
falling into the cultivation of regrets, all of it with—in the back of our cursed
self-reflective mind—the inescapable awareness of our own transiency, the
awareness of the irremediable fact that we are going to vanish from this life,
eternally severed from all of our embodied attachments.

Index

For the benefit of digital users, indexed terms that span two pages (e.g., 52–53) may, on occasion, appear on only one of those pages.

Figures are indicated by f following the page number

perversion, 155–56
phonemic discrimination, 131–32
potlatch rituals, 137
preferences/attractions shaping, 20–21
prejudice, essentialism and, 95–98, 119
pretense, 122
pride, 114
pride/loyalty, 5–6, 19, 99, 100, 118
Primo Levi Center, 39
privilege awareness, 5
pseudo beliefs, 123–25, 129
punishments, 66, 139–40, 156–58

Rahami, Ahmad, xiii–xiv, xvi
Ramayana, 142, 143, 144
recognition (reputation), 11, 24, 32, 51–52, 59–60, 62, 96, 104–5, 134–35
reconciliation of facts *vs.* experience, xiv–xv, 31, 32–33, 102
reconciliation of values, 11–16
recursive thinking, 111–13, 122–23
reflective abstraction, 111–13
revenge/retaliation, 156–58
roles, juggling of, 42–44
Romania, 51

Sahli, Yassin, 101–2
Samoa, 66, 78, 138, 147–49, 150–51
Sartre, Jean Paul, 6
school shooters, 25–26
Schopenhauer, Arthur, 90–91
selectivity, 125–27
self-assertion, 118–19
self-attributes, 116–18
self-conceptualizing in children, 119–21
self-consciousness, 3–6, 59–60, 64, 104–5, 109–15, 122–23, 144–46, 155
self-delusion, 111, 116–21
self-essentialism, 104–6
self-esteem, 117, 120, 121
self-identity, 58–60
self-image/self-branding, 105–6, 112–13
self-protection, xiii, 16, 159
self-reflective curse, 3–6
self-sacrifice, 137–40
self-unity, ix, 18, 32
Sengoku jidai, 143–44
sense of self. *See* self-consciousness

separation anxiety, 64
serial killers, 11–12, 14–15, 25–26, 32, 65
Shadenfreude, 154
shame/guilt, 5–6, 19, 31, 66, 113, 118, 149
Shieffelin, Edward, 146–47
Shinto, 87
Shore, Bradd, 78, 151
Simmel, Marianne, 75–76
Simpson, O. J., 14–15
Sironi, Françoise, 39–40, 47–48
slavery, 7–8
social clustering, 79–82, 88–89, 90–94
social cognition, 112–13
social-cognitive achievements, 114–15
social collaboration, 34–35
social deception, 14–15
social exclusion, 66
social identity, 120–21
social isolation, 63–64
solitary confinement, 66
sphere/moral code collapse, 39–41
spherical alliances. *See* alliances
Spitz, René, 63
staging by imitation. *See* mimesis
stereotype threat, 80
stereotyping, 23, 79–82, 88, 90–91, 95–98
still face phenomenon, 125–27
subjective experience, 18–19
suicide, 3
Summers, Larry, 80–81, 83
symbolic functioning, 6, 21, 31, 33–34, 50–51, 62–63, 64, 66, 86, 94, 95, 96, 99–101, 109–10, 111, 113, 122–23, 125, 128, 134–35, 150, 155

tale of the chameleon, 41
Taylor, Charles, xv–xvi, xv–xvi n.5, 83–84
theories of mind, 15, 123–24, 125–27
thinging/ideology, 86–89, 104–6.
See also essentialism
Tibet, 139
torturers/victims of torture, 39–41, 47–48, 52–53
totalitarianism, 84–85
tragic flaws, 141
Treaty of Versailles, 26–27
truth, 125